Napoleon's
Imperial Guard

Napoleon's
Imperial Guard
From Marengo to Waterloo

J. T. Headley

LEONAUR

Napoleon's Imperial Guard: from Marengo to Waterloo
by J. T. Headley

Published by Leonaur Ltd

Material original to this edition and the text in this form
copyright © 2007 Leonaur Ltd

ISBN: 978-1-84677-301-3 (hardcover)
ISBN: 978-1-84677-302-0 (softcover)

http://www.leonaur.com

Publisher's Note

Contents

Introduction

The present work lays no claim to originality. It is also without pretension, being designed as a simple history of the Imperial Guard of Napoleon.

The materials for it were mostly collected in the preparation of my "Napoleon and his Marshals," and hence it was comparatively an easy task to arrange them in a connected and intelligible form. At first sight there might seem to be a good deal of repetition of scenes described in that work, because reference is necessarily made to them. But what in the former work is a mere reference made to give a right conception of a battle or campaign, in this becomes a full and detailed account. In the former the main features of a conflict are delineated, and the conduct of the Guard only mentioned incidentally, while in the latter the battle-field and the main operations of the army are sketched only enough to allow the introduction of the Guard upon the scene. So that while the reference to the same things are constant, the details are entirely different. Two or three exceptions to this remark occur in the present work, but I thought that the reader in these cases would prefer a repetition to a hiatus in the history of the Guard.

I believe there is a description of but a single battle in the whole book, although the conduct of the Guard in action and its heavy onsets are of course necessarily dwelt upon. Still it is meant to be rather a domestic than military history. Judging by my own feelings, I thought there were many who having always taken a deep interest in the recital of its deeds would be glad to know more of its formation, internal arrangements, and by what moral and other means it became such a terrible corps. I have been as much interested in the social private life as in its public conduct, and dwelt with more pleasure upon those incidents and anecdotes illustrating its sense of honor, noble pride, and steadfast integrity, than in the march of its iron columns through smoke and fire to victory. I believe that others will feel the same.

The facts are taken from a variety of works which I need not here enumerate. The statistics, however, and most of the details exhibiting the private life, if I may so term it, of the Guard, are taken from a French work entitled, "Historie Polulaire de la Garde Imperiale, par Emile Marco de Saint Hiliare." It is a large work, comprising some five hundred closely printed pages. I should have given credit to it in the body of my work, since many scenes are in fact translations condensed, by the references would have been endless. I have used it without stint. The illustrations are mostly taken from it.

To those who doubted my statements respecting the origin of the wars of France, in my "Napoleon and his Marshals," I submit, with the earnest wish it should receive their careful attention, the last chapter in this work.

CHAPTER 1

The Old Guard

The Imperial Guard—or so it is more familiarly known, the Old Guard of Napoleon, is as much renowned in modern as the Greek Phalanx was in ancient war. When the latter, eight or sixteen thousand strong, shoulder to shoulder, and shield touching shield, moved sixteen deep on the enemy, the battle was over. So when the eagles of the Old Guard were seen advancing through the smoke of the conflict, the result was no longer doubtful. Its whole history is an illustration of the moral and physical power which a great idea imparts.

Called upon only in great emergencies, it came to regard itself as the prop of the empire. When its columns were ordered to move to the attack, every soldier knew it was not to execute a manoeuvre, or perform a subordinate part in the battle, but to march where the struggle was deadliest, and the fate of the army was to be decided. He knew, too, that over the dead and dying, over flaming batteries, and through ranks of steel, the steady battalions were to go. The bugle was never to sound a retreat for him and no reserve help him sustain the shock. It was the consciousness of this great responsibility that made it great and irresistible. This idea alone filled the mind, leaving no room for fear of death. The bearskin caps of the grenadiers were never seen advancing to the charge without causing a shout from the whole army. The force it possessed over others was as much moral as physical. Beaten troops rallied at its approach, and despair gave way to confidence, and the cry of terror was changed into the shout of victory. The enemy on the other hand when they saw the deep and massive columns of the Guard approaching, were already half beaten. The prestige of victory that went with its eagles paralyzed their arms, and they struggled against hope. So well known was it when they were ordered up, that the final hour of one or the other army had come, that the contest along the different portions of the line became apparently of no account, and everything waited the result of their shock. So perfect was their discipline, that their treat was unlike that of other regiments, while the consciousness of their power gave a grandeur to their movements, no body of men in ancient or modern times have possessed. Their bivouac at night and their squares in position on the battle-field, were always the great objects of interest, for they enfolded the emperor. Napoleon loved them devotedly, and always called them his children. They never suffered while anything was to be had, and he would listen kindly to the suit of the meanest soldier. And well did they deserve his love. For him, they knew no weariness or pain. His presence amid them compensated for all losses; and at his voice, and for his welfare, they would move steadily and cheerfully on death. The care he took of them, and the pride he felt in them, and the glory with which he covered them, naturally produced a strong and abiding attachment. He was proud of their appearance, and always gave them a prominent place in his great exhibitions at Paris. He allowed liberally for the expenditures of their officers, wishing them to be dressed magnificently, although habited himself in the plainest costume. The dress of the drum-major of the Foot Grenadiers alone cost $6000. So richly worked in gold was it, that in 1809, when the Old Guard made its triumphant entry into Vienna, the ladies said, that the drum-major would make a more profitable prisoner than Napoleon. Even the musicians and surgeons were dressed in this sumptuous uniform. The gorgeous appearance of the chief officers contrasted well with the grave, austere costume of the battalions of the Guard. When in front of their lines, the former appeared like the sparkling foam and crest of the wave that swept darkly after.

Napoleon took an interest in everything pertaining to the officers of his Guard, even their marriages. He was not less solicitous they should be good citizens than good officers. One day, Dorsenne having expressed some astonishment at this paternal solicitude, especially in regard to the approaching marriage of an officer, Napoleon replied, "Are you not all lions? Very well, it is important the race should not perish. France and myself will have need of new claws and new teeth, when yours can no longer serve us." The same interest extended to the children of those who fell in battle. They were provided for and well educated. Speaking once to Davoust, of the reluctance of the soldiers of the Guard, to leave it even for promotion among the troops of the line, he said, "My old soldiers had rather eat a piece of bread near me, than a chicken a hundred leagues from my person. It is true that if they are not able to leave me, it also gives me great pain to part from them." He inquired into the wants of the soldiers, and often playfully asked them, "My grumblers, are you in want of anything?" The uniform answer was "nothing." The discipline was very severe, and the least departure from duty was visited with punishment. It was more rigorous than in the army of the line. Napoleon had said, "If I wished only intrepid men, I could take at hazard the first soldiers in the army I came to, but I deserve more, I want good conduct, morality and obedience, and this I find difficult." These words were often commented on in the Guard, and cases of punishment were rare. Absence when the morning roll was called was punished with two days in the hall of police; absence at the evening roll, four days in the hall of police, and eight days of constant duty; sleeping away from his quarters, fifteen days in the hall of police, and a month of constant duty; drunkenness and insubordination brought the dungeon, and a repetition of the offense, expulsion from the corps. Even when out of their barracks, the hand of discipline was on them. They were forbidden to promenade with suspected women, and haunting bad places and taverns. They were not allowed to walk in the Palais Royal. In the day-time they might cross the garden, if in their route, but in the night, never. Their amusements naturally took a simple and innocent direction, their manners grew polite and affable, so that they became examples of good behavior in the midst of a turbulent population. Even on fête days, when great license was allowed, they were quiet in their deportments, and subdued in their mirth, as though it became them who held so high a trust, and so marked a position, to be reserved and composed. Each man seemed to feel that the honor of the whole corps was entrusted to his keeping. This sentiment and thought pervading every heart imparted that steady valor and unwavering constancy amid the dispirited and flying army, fast perishing in the snows of Russia. It is a singular fact, that for fourteen years, Napoleon did not expel a single officer of any grade from the Guard.

He wished it to be an example to the rest of the army, and so it was in discipline, obedience, good behavior and heroic courage. It was on this account that a duel among its officers always threw him into a great rage, as indeed a duel among any of his officers. During the campaign in Egypt, Junot, his first aid-de-camp and Lannes, fought a bloody duel, in which the former received a frightful sabre cut, which well nigh sent him to his grave, and the latter had his head nearly opened. When Desgenettes informed Napoleon of it, he was furious. What!" he exclaimed, "do they wish to cut each other's throats. They have been among the reeds of the Nile to dispute with the crocodiles for the palm of ferocity, and to leave them the corpse of him who should be slain? Have they not enough of the Arabs and the plague? They deserve that I should call them before me, and that. . . . " And then after a moment of silence, he added, "No, I do not wish to see them. I do not wish any one even to speak to me of them."

The severe manner in which he vented his displeasure against Filangieri, the godson of his sister, for killing General Franceschetti, was well known, and duels after a while became a rare occurrence among the officers of the Guard. One harmless duel ending in a farce never came to his ears. It has been published as having occurred between two Spanish officers, whereas, the true heroes of it were to captains of the horse grenadiers of the Guard. One of them had spoken in a light, joking manner to the sister of the other. The latter demanded that an apology should be made to her in presence of the assembled family. The former refused, and a challenge was the consequence. They met in the woods of Boulogne, and had already drawn their swords, when a laboring man, till then unnoticed, advanced, and addressing the combatants in a piteous tone said:

"Alas! my dear officers, I am a poor joiner without work, and the father of a family."

"Eh, my brave fellow," said one of the seconds, "retire,

this is no time to ask for alms; do you not see that these gentlemen are about to cut each other's throats?"

"It is for that reason, my brave officers," he replied, "that I have come to ask the preference."

"What preference?" they exclaimed.

"To make the coffins of these two gentlemen, for I am a poor joiner without work, and the father of a family." At these words, the two antagonists paused, and gazed on each other a moment, then burst into a simultaneous peal of laughter. Their anger was over, and advancing, they shook hands, and then retired to a restaurant to finish their quarrel with forks over a well-covered table.

No matter who was the victor in a duel, Napoleon always punished the challenger. "A duel," he was wont to say, "is no indication of courage—it is the fury of a cannibal."

The same rigor was shown to every departure from duty. Thus more by internal regulations than outward forms, did he gradually perfect the character of the Guard. By visiting with displeasure acts which did not come under the rules of military discipline, he taught them to curb their passions, and show an example of uprightness and integrity as well as bravery to the army. The soldiers of it received extra pay, and especial favors were lavished on them by Napoleon. This he knew would not be borne by the rest of the army, unless deserved not only by superior service but a higher character. Never pillaging a conquered city, or giving way to the license of a common soldier, while quartered in, the latter naturally regarded them as superior—as occupying a rank above them, akin to that of an officer. Napoleon said, he would not be disquieted by the conduct of soldiers attached to his person.

So strict was their integrity and so nice their sense of honor, that in every city occupied by the French troops, they left more or less grateful recollections of themselves among

A Chasseur á Cheval of the Imperial Guard

the inhabitants. Their upright deportment and conciliatory behavior were remembered long after; for on Napoleon's final abdication, these veterans distributed themselves over the world, and received kindnesses from the very countries they had swept through as conquerors.

So in garrison, at home, instead of being riotous and quarrelsome, they prevented quarrels among the citizens, and left behind them the esteem and good will of all.

The character of the Old Guard, as delineated above, was the result of education and discipline. It required time to perfect it, but after it was formed it distinguished this renowned corps to the last. I have been thus particular in describing its moral qualities because they are less known—its deeds shall illustrate its military character.

In Bonaparte's first campaign in Italy, he had simply his staff about him. In Egypt, a corps which he named guides, acted as a personal guard, most of whom returned with him to France, at length became incorporated in the Guard. He said that a narrow escape from being once made prisoner in Italy, suggested to him the organization of this corps.

A national and imperial Guard have been common to all monarchial and despotic governments. France had the former during the revolution. It was on this Bonaparte thundered with his cannon, when he quelled the sections. He was then at the head of the Guard of the Convention, a corps formed to protect that body from the violence of the mob. It was composed of four companies, united in a single battalion, with sappers, drummers, and a band of musicians; and numbered at first, officers and all, but five hundred men. In it; however, were the young Murat, Lefebvre, Guisard, Monnet, and many others who afterwards attained high rank and renown. Robespierre, Couthon, St. Just, and others, had their creatures in the ranks, and it was a miserable, inefficient corps. After the death of the former, the Convention purged it thoroughly of its bad members, and added to it men of a different stamp, so that when Bonaparte put himself at its head to quell the revolt of the sections, he found it, especially the grenadiers, a warlike and well-disciplined body of soldiers.

After the overthrow of the Convention, and the establishment of the Directory, the Guard of the Convention became the Guard of the Executive Directory. An order was issued fixing its number at a hundred and twenty foot soldiers, and a hundred and twenty cavalry. The Directory also continued the work of purgation, and incorporated into the corps, the veterans of the Rhine, Sambre-et-Meuse, Pyrenees and Italy. A severe discipline was introduced, and soon, under the instructions of men, who had learned the art of war on the field of battle, became one of the finest regiments of the army.

When Bonaparte plotted the overthrow of the Directory, he introduced emissaries into the Guard, who soon worked the soldiers over to the interests of their future master, so that when Moulin, one of the Directors, endeavored to rouse them in defence of the government, they quietly remained in their barracks. One the 20th Brumaire, when Bonaparte was saluted First Consul by the people, he went to the Place de Carrousel, at the head of a magnificent staff, to review the regiments that formed the garrison of Paris. The Guard of the Directory formed the right of the line of battle, and as Bonaparte halted in front of it, he announced that, in future it was to be called the "Guard of the Consuls." Long live General Bonaparte, rent the air along the whole line, and the Imperial Guard was born.

This was the nucleus of the Consular Guard, which in the end, became the famed Imperial Guard, whose name sent terror over Europe. The change that immediately passed over this corps, was indicative of the future plans of its chief. From two companies, comprising 270 men, it was raised to 2089 men, divided into one company of light infantry; two battalions of foot grenadiers; one company of horse chasseurs; two squadrons of cavalry; one company of light artillery, of which a third was mounted.

It may be of interest to some to see the first organization of this famed guard:

Staff Officers of the Commander - 71
Inferior Officers of Infantry - 17
2 Battalions of Grenadiers - 1,188
1 Company of Chasseurs - 99
Superior Officers of Cavalry - 19
2 Squadrons of Grenadiers - 468
Company of Horse Chasseurs - 117
10 D. of Artillery - 110
Total, 2,089

This is the number as fixed by the decree of the Consuls. Only a small portion of these, however, was given to Consul Bonaparte as General of the army.

When he took the bold resolution to make the Tuileries his palace, the first thing he did in the morning, was to review the Consular Guard, and the half brigades, which were still in barracks in Paris. Passing through their ranks, he addressed flattering words to the chief officers of the corps, and then placing himself before the pavilion of the clock, with Murat on his right and Lannes on his left, and behind him a numerous staff of young warriors, bronzed by the sun of Italy and Egypt, he saw the troops defile before him. As the standards of the 96th, 43d and 30th demi-brigades saluted him, presenting nothing but shreds of banners riddled with balls and blackened with powder, he raised his chapeau, and bowed in token of respect. The shout that followed rocked the old palace to its foundations. The troops having passed, he mounted with a bold step the stairs of the

Tuileries, that none but a king ever before dared to occupy. It was a hazardous move on the part of the young chief of the republic, thus to foreshadow his future designs. He felt it to be such, and to offset this assumption of regal splendor, a few days after he issued the following decree to the Consular Guard, "Washington is dead! This great man has fought against tyranny, and consolidated the liberty of his country. His memory will always be dear to the French people, as to all free men in both hemispheres, and especially to the French soldiers, who, equally with the American soldiers, fight for liberty and equality. The First Consul, therefore, decrees that for ten days black crape shall be hung on the standards and colors of the Consular Guard."

The distribution of "arms of honor," in reward for great deeds, was also very popular, and prepared the way for the future creation of the "Legion of Honor."

A third incident helped to increase the popular enthusiasm for Napoleon, and to attach the Guard still more strongly to him. A sergeant of grenadiers, who was noted for the remarkable feats in arms he had performed, received one of these "arms of honor," a fine sabre. Immediately on its reception, he wrote the following naive letter to the First Consul, in which, it will be observed, he forgets to thank his benefactor for the gift, and simply enumerates his own deeds and asks a favor. It commences:

Leon Aune

Sergeant of Grenadiers in the 32d demi-brigade

To citizen Bonaparte, First Consul at Paris.

Citizen First Consul: Your arrival upon the territory of the Republic has consoled all pure souls, chiefly mine. Having no hope but in you, I come to you as my guardian deity, to pray to you to give a place in your good memory to Leon, whom you have so often loaded with favors on the field of battle.

Not having been able to embark with you for Egypt, there to reap new laurels under your command, I find myself at the depot of the 32d demi-brigade, in the quality of a sergeant. Having been told by my comrades, that you often spoke of me in Egypt, I pray you not to abandon me, while you make me know that you remember me. It is useless to remind you of affairs, where I have shown myself a true republican, and where I have merited the esteem of my superiors. Nevertheless, you will not forget that at Montenotte, I saved the life of General Rampon, and the Chief of the Brigade, Masse, as they will certify. At Diego, I took a stand of colors from the Chief Engineer of the Army of the enemy; at Lodi, I was the first to mount to the assault, and I opened the gates to our brethren in arms; at Borghetto, I was among the first who passed the bridges—the bridge giving way, I was cast among the enemy, and took the commandant of the post prisoner. A little after, being made prisoner myself, I slew the hostile commanding officer, and by this action, rescued four hundred more prisoners, like myself, and enabled them to re-join their respective corps. Moreover, I have five wounds upon my body. I dare then to hope, and am well persuaded, that you will always have regard for those who have so well served their country.

Health and respect,

Leon Aune

This letter, more distinguished, we must confess for its simplicity and honesty, than for its modesty, furnished Bonaparte, an admirable opportunity for producing an effect upon his Guard, and indeed the whole army. He intended his answer should be made public, although apparently written as a private note. He wrote—

I have received your letter, my brave comrade. You did not need to refresh my memory; you are the bravest grenadier, since the death of Benezete; you have had one of the sabres that I have distributed to the army. All your comrades, with one accord, pronounce you worthy of it above all others. I desire much to see you; the Minister of War, sends an order for you to come to Paris.

Bonaparte

The sensation this letter caused in the army was prodigious. What, the First Consul of the Republic, and the greatest General of modern times, write to a common sergeant, and call him "my brave comrade!" He might occupy forth Tuileries with the pomp of an emperor, such language would atone for all in the sight of the army. A better republican could not exist. This letter was a double hit, for it not only removed from the soldiers whatever suspicions might have arisen of Bonaparte's designs, when they saw him ascend the steps of the Tuileries, as its occupant, but it fired them with the loftiest enthusiasm. Who would not fight bravely under a chieftain who bestowed such epithets on the humblest soldier for deeds of daring?

But Bonaparte's chief favors were lavished on his Guard. Already he seemed to forecast the future, and see the terrible corps with which he was to surround his person. This attention to his guard soon produced feelings of envy and rivalry in other regiments of the army, which at length broke out into quarrels and serious conflicts. One day a trumpeter of the mounted chasseurs of the Guard was conversing at the entrance to the barracks with some under-officers like himself, when several masters of arms in the army of the line approached and demanded to see their colleagues—the masters of arms of the chasseurs, intending it as an insult to the trumpeter and his friends. "They rest in Egypt," was the reply. "But, trumpeter," said one, as he gave his moustache a contemptuous twist, "you ought to have some one of them remaining." The trumpeter replying in the negative, the masters showed so clearly that they were bent on a quarrel, that the former became impatient and exclaimed, "Oh, well, gentlemen, enter the barracks, shut your eyes, and the first man you put your hands on will prove to you that, if the masters and provosts of the regiment rest in Egypt, their good swords yet remain." This was sufficient; each chose his champion, and, in a few minutes, four masters of arms were put hors du combat. Eugene Beauharnais, who was then but chief of a squadron of chasseurs, hearing of it, called the trumpeter to him and reproached him bitterly. The latter defended himself on the ground that he was provoked into a quarrel. "I detest bullies," broke in Eugene, with a tone that did not admit a reply. "Let me hear no more of such scandalous conduct. As to you, if it happens again, I will put a blade of wood in your scabbard." "My commander," said the trumpeter, smiling, "there will still be means to brush the clothes of those who would throw dirt upon ours."

A few days after, new provocations were given to the chasseurs of the Guard, when a quarrel ensued which finally drew fifty men into a deliberate fight. Murderous work would have followed had not Lefebvre, who had been apprised of it, charged on them with a squadron of horse grenadiers.

These quarrels, however, were soon forgotten in more serious events, and the Consular Guard was to place itself beyond the reach of envy and be looked up to as a model, and not frowned upon as a rival. The peace was over, and Bonaparte directed his vast energies, which had been employed in developing the resources of the nation, to the war which threatened him on every side. The campaign of Marengo was at hand.

CHAPTER 2

Marengo

During Bonaparte's campaign in Egypt, France had lost her possessions in Italy; and, after his return, he determined to make that country again the field of his conquests.

One hardly knows which to wonder at most, the resurrection he gave to France in the few months that succeeded his election as First Consul; the development of her internal resources and strength, or the magical army that seemed to rise at his touch from the earth, and the next moment hang in three mighty columns amid the glaciers of the Alps. As in his expedition to Egypt he had completely outwitted both England and the Continent, which remained to the last moment ignorant of the destination of his army, so now he managed to mislead Europe as to the point where he designed to strike. It was generally supposed that he was on his way to Genoa, to relieve Massena, who was starving to death within its walls. That brave veteran thought so too, and long and patiently waited to hear the thunder of his cannon, amid the Appenines. But Bonaparte was seeking the Austrian general, Melas, though, strange as it may seem, when he had reunited his divisions in the plains of Piedmont he could not find him. It was owing to this ignorance of the whereabouts of Melas that his army became so divided. Having scoured the plains of Marengo, of which a few months before he had spoken as the spot for a great battle, without finding the enemy, he supposed he must have taken flight. He never dreamed that if he intended to give battle at all, he would leave the plain—above all the village of Marengo unoccupied. He, therefore, left Victor with two divisions at Marengo, and Lannes with one division en echelon in the plain, and hastened back to his head quarters at Voghera, hoping to hear news of the enemy from Moncey on the Tessino, or Duhesme, on the Lower Po. Luckily for him, however, the Scrivia had overflowed its banks, so that he was compelled to stop on the other side. Despatches were received from these officers, stating that all was quiet in their sections. He then decided that Melas must have gone by way of Novi to Genoa, and despatched Desaix with a single division, to intercept him.

Great was his surprise, therefore, in the morning, when a courier from Victor, burst in a wild gallop, into Torre di Garlfolo, announcing that the whole Austrian army was crossing the Bormida and marching straight upon Marengo. Victor had scarcely sent off his despatch before the enemy, 40,000 strong, sustained by two hundred pieces of artillery, was upon him. Sixteen thousand men were all he had, with which to oppose this formidable array. But for the little muddy stream of Fontenone, along whose banks he had placed his army, the battle would have been irretrievably lost, long before Bonaparte could arrive. As it was, nothing but the most stubborn resolution held that ground. Immense batteries thundered on his shivering lines, almost within pistol shot, making horrible gaps at every discharge. His ranks melted away around him like men of mist, still he maintained his ground, anxiously waiting the arrival of Bonaparte. If he could not hold that position he was lost, for nothing by the little village of Marengo lay between him and the vast open plain, where the cavalry of the enemy would scatter his army like dust before the wind. For two mortal hours did he stand on the edge of that narrow stream and see his army sink, whole ranks at a time, before the murderous discharges of artillery. One division, stationed in the open field, was almost entirely annihilated by grape shot. At length the Austrians forced the stream. The French commanders put forth almost superhuman efforts, to stop the flow of troops across it. But they were compelled to retire, leaving the field heaped with the dead. The road was filled with wounded and disbanded soldiers, the latter crying that all was lost. Lannes, though outflanked, was making desperate efforts to hold on with his wing to Marengo, his last remaining hope. Retreat was impossible, it would become a slaughter in the open plain. Pressed by that mass of artillery, and chased by clouds of cavalry, his beaten, and already half destroyed division, would be crushed to atoms.

This was the state of things at ten o'clock, when Bonaparte came on a full gallop to the field. As soon as he received Victor's despatch, he sent for Desaix, and taking with him a single division and his Consular Guard, set off; a reserve of cavalry was to follow. Casting his eye over the disastrous field, he saw but the shattered and flying remnant of the army, but he also saw, at a glance, that where Lannes still held Marengo, was his only hope. He must there make a stand and rally his troops in the rear. It was then he rode up to the Consular Guard, and bade them march into the open plain and hold the cavalry of the enemy in check. These eight hundred forming instantly into a square, moved forward and presented their wall-like sides to the Austrian horse. In the meantime Bonaparte flew with his fresh troops to the help of Lannes. As the wearied soldiers of the latter saw the escort that told of the approach of their commander, they sent up a loud shout, and rushed with renewed fury to the assault. Lannes performed prodigies; and at first, success smiled on the efforts of Bonaparte—but at length overborne by superior numbers, he was compelled to retreat. Then came a trial to which all the rest, murderous as it had been, was as nothing. To move into the open plain, pressed by a victorious army, with such heavy artillery and numerous cavalry, was testing the nerves of officers and men to the utmost.

Yet all this time the Consular Guard remained unshaken. "A living citadel" it moved over the plain, rolling from its adamantine sides the successive waves of cavalry that dashed against them. Bonaparte's eye often turned anxiously to it. At moments it would be lost to view, apparently engulfed by the enemy. The dark mass that shut it in, would then rend asunder, and there moved that wall-like enclosure, the fire pouring in streams from its sides. Lannes fought like a lion, carrying his squares slowly and sternly over the plain, though eighty pieces of artillery hurled their iron storm upon his mutilated ranks.

The Consular Guard till now had been attacked only by cavalry. It seemed impossible that so small a body of men, forming but a mere speck on that vast plain, could resist the overwhelming squadrons. Astonished at such resistance, the enemy at length brought forward his artillery. Round and grape shot smote through the thinned ranks till it was supposed they were so dreadfully shaken that the cavalry could ride them down with ease, when they were ordered again to charge. Advancing on a sweeping gallop, they burst with redoubled fury upon this mere handful of men. Again and again they thundered on that firm formation, but when the dust and smoke cleared away there it stood solid and terrible as ever. Recoil and melt away it must, and did, but break or fly it never would. In the midst of a vast plain, surrounded by tens of thousands of men and horses, pressed by a victorious foe, enveloped in dark masses of cavalry that kept falling in successive shocks on its exhausted ranks, rent by cannon shot—in the intervals of the roars of artillery their ears assailed by cries of terror from their flying comrades—ignorant how the battle was going in other parts of the disordered field, save that the whole army was in full retreat, this band of eight hundred men, now reduced to a mere handful, never thought of flying.

In the midst of this tumult and carnage, when they seemed no longer struggling for victory, and intent only on showing how brave men should die, a sight burst on them that filled every heart with the wildest enthusiasm. As the cloud of battle rent a moment before them, they saw in the midst of the turbulent plain, Napoleon, surrounded by his staff and two hundred mounted grenadiers, bravely breasting the storm. At the view an involuntary and frantic hurrah burst from that solid square, and "vive Napoleon," rolled over the field like the shout of victory.

That single square, though dreadfully narrowed, and bleeding at every pore remained as perfect in its formation at the close of that disastrous retreat, as when it first marched into the plain to stem the tide of battle. To use the expressive metaphor of Bonaparte, it stood, during those five hours of slaughter, a "column of granite."

The arrival of Desaix, and the defeat of the Austrians, are well known. Italy was reconquered. Bonaparte, after the battle, addressing Bessieres, who commanded the guard, said, "The Guard which you command is covered with glory." The lesson he learned that day was not lost upon him. He saw what could be done with a body of picked men, bound to him with affection, and borne up with the consciousness of the high trust committed to their charge. Such men were irresistible.

This was the first baptism of the Guard, and a more bloody one it could not well have had.

MARENGO

Lannes, as a reward for his bravery, was appointed commander of it. In November of the next year, 1801, however, it underwent a change, and four general officers were appointed over it. General Davoust for the Foot Grenadiers, General Soult for the Foot Chasseurs, Bessieres for the Cavalry, and Mortier for the Artillery and Matelots.

Lannes, of course, lost his command which he had so nobly earned, some say because he managed the chest of the Guard loosely, and rendered false accounts of the money he received. This is doubtful, still he lived in the most prodigal manner, and expended more than he was authorized to do, thus setting an example which would not answer in the commander of a Guard, whose character Bonaparte had determined should be without reproach. Others attributed his dismissal to his too great familiarity of manner. The dignity of the First Consul could not permit that freedom from his first lieutenants, which the extravagant notions of equality then pervading the army, sanctioned. Lannes and Augereau, blunt and republican in their habits and thoughts, often took unwarrantable liberties with Bonaparte, relying on their great deeds to screen them from rebuke. It is said that a short time previous to the new appointments in the Guard, as Bonaparte one day ordered some Barbary horses, which had been sent to him as a present, to be brought into the court of Malmaison, Lannes, who was present, proposed a game of billiards, the stake to be the price of one of the horses. Bonaparte consented; they played and Lannes won. The former, no doubt, designed he should, making use of the proposal of his brave lieutenant to bestow on him a favor.

"I have beaten thee," said the latter, (for he was accustomed to thee and thou Bonaparte like a quaker,) and of course I have the right of choice," and without waiting for permission, he ran out and examined the horses, and having selected the most beautiful, put on the saddle and bridle, and springing into the seat, spurred away at a gallop saying, "Adieu, Bonaparte, I will not dine here to-day, for if I remain thou wilt succeed in getting back thy horse." Napoleon did not esteem his Ajax any the less for this; he knew his brave heart too well, but he saw that the repetition of such scenes would weaken his authority and prevent the absolute submission to his will which he required of the Guard. Lannes was sent ambassador to Lisbon.

1802, 1803, AND A PART OF 1804

Bonaparte soon issued a new decree respecting the Guard, augmenting it still more. Among other changes he made soldier of the drivers of the artillery wagons. Upheld by no feeling of honor and subject to no promotion, however daring they might be in carrying the guns into the enemy's fire, they at the moment the action became hot, would cut the traces and gallop off. Bonaparte decreed that they should wear the uniform of the soldiers and be incorporated into the army. He decreed also that the whole military force should be called upon to furnish recruits whenever needed to the Guard—their admission in it to be the reward of bravery and good conduct. Several qualifications were necessary to render a soldier a fit candidate. He must be in active service, he must have made at least four campaigns, obtained rewards for deeds of arms or noble conduct, or been wounded. The grenadiers must be at least five feet six inches high, and the chasseurs five feet four inches, and each one to have maintained an irreproachable character.

An incident occurred at this time which shows how sensitive Bonaparte was to the least demoralizing influence in his Guard. Two grenadiers having committed suicide, he added the following note to the order of the day, "The grenadier Gabon has committed suicide from disappointment in love; he was in other respects a good subject. This is the second event of the kind that has happened to the corps in a month. The First Consul ordains that it shall be affixed to the order of the Guard that a soldier ought to know how to overcome the grief and melancholy arising from his passions; that to bear with constancy the pains of the soul, shows as much true courage as to rest fixed and immovable under the fire of a battery. To abandon one's self to chagrin without resistance, to slay one's self to get rid of it, is to desert the battle-field before the victory."

It was by such means he taught those who were in future to serve him with blind devotion, never asking or caring what were his orders, that self-endurance and heroic resolution which, years after, in the snows of Russia, astonished the world.

THE IMPERIAL GUARD, 1804

After various political changes, Bonaparte was at length declared emperor. The decree of the 10th Thermidor, 29th of July, was simply added, "The Consular Guard will take in future the name of the Imperial Guard, and will continue to be specially attached to my person."

Soon after he began to introduce changes in the uniform of the Guard. The first innovation was a bold push, laughable from its insignificance, but withal, a serious matter; this was no less than to dispense with their long queues and long hair of which they were so proud and tenacious as the Germans and Gauls, according to Tacitus, were in the time of Caesar.

One day after a review of the troops, Napoleon standing in the hall of the Marshals, surrounded by the chiefs of the separate corps, broke out into one of those biting sarcasms which so often made those wince who heard them. He began with the hats. "Decidedly, gentlemen," said he, "I do not wish to see my troops any more wear the chapeaux. It is always placed on their head in such a manner as to make a gutter of one corner. It is as disagreeable to the sight as injurious to the health of the soldier. It is ridiculous in a day of rain or great head, or as to-day when we have had both together; to see a soldier with the collar of his coat covered with a white paste, his hair badly held together by an equivocal riband, his forehead and cheeks running with a milky water, and the whole covered with a narrow hat, badly shaped, which protects the face from neither rain nor sun! One needs only to see them in Italy and Egypt. Poor devils, I suffered for them." One of the officers hinted at an ordinance, when Napoleon broke out again, winding up with an attack on "long tresses and useless queues." "How, sire," exclaimed the same officer, "would you shear all without distinction," "Yes sir," he replied, "like sheep." The former suggested that it would be impossible to obtain the consent of the officers to such a change, so attached were they to their locks. A glance of fire was the reply, as he exclaimed, "I should like to see, Monsious Colonel, the men who owe everything to me, my soldiers, in a word, to reflect on the thing at all, is it not sufficient that I wish it? Is it for my Guard to object when I require that all should have their hair shorn?" Passing his hand quickly over his own head, he added, "Do I wear a queue, is not my hair cut close?" "Yes," said Junot, "and the soldiers of the Guard call you nothing by the "little shorn"—le petit tondu.

Napoleon smiled in spite of himself, and said, "very well, the more reason—a soldier should always follow the example of his chief. I am aware that some fop or Adonis of an officer will not be very well satisified; but those who will not be content. . . . " He left the sentence unfinished, and crossing his hands behind him, promenaded awhile in silence, in the circle of officers that surrounded him. At length he said, "I will speak to Berrieres and Murat about it, I will commence by demanding Murat to sacrifice that head of hair a la Louis XIV., which, with our habits and military costume is ridiculous. The chiefs of the army must show examples of obedience. I wish neither tresses nor queues nor powder nor pomatum." Saying this he bowed and passed out.

The same day Murat who had assisted at the review of the morning, coming to receive the orders of the Emperor, asked if he had been pleased with the review. "Yes," said Napoleon, but (fixing his eyes on the long hair of his beautiful brother-in- law) added, "I should have been pleased if you had cut off all the tresses and queues of your cavaliers." Murat said nothing, but bowed and disappeared among the crowd of officers that were assembling. He saw at once that the reign of queues was over. At the extremity of the gallery he met Bessieres, one of the kfour commanders of the Guard, whose immense queue was a subject of remark throughout the whole army. "Eh bien, my dear fellow," said he in a tone half sorrowful and half joking, "thou hast heard the words of the Emperor—no more queues! Accept in advance my condolence on the approaching fall of yours." "My dear sir," replied the young marshal, "the roots of a queue like mine reach near to the heart, and the Emperor with all his power cannot make me cut it off. I hope our old comrades of Italy and Egypt will prove refractory as myself in this matter."

The next day Napoleon spoke again to Murat, who although he sympathized with Bessieres, did not dare to express his sentiments. At length turning towards him, the Emperor said laconically, "My Guard alone shall wear the queue, and it shall not be more than two inches long, such shall be the ordinance."

The reign of queues was over; the young officers adopted the change cheerfully, and on the day of the publication of the ordinance, the barbers' shops near the quarters of the troops were filled from morning till night, and more than two thousand queues were sacrificed. But in the same evening there were more than twenty duels. A quarrel commenced by one calling another just sheared, a spaniel. Friends on either side, took part in it, till the whole corps was involved, and, for awhile, serious difficulty was threatened. It required great tact to settle quietly the rage caused by this onslaught against tresses and queues.

Shearing of the Guard

An appropriate uniform for every portion of the Guard was adopted and it soon reached that eminence and deserved the character given of it in the preceding chapter.

Each of the corps of foot and mounted grenadiers and chasseurs of the Guard furnished a battalion and squadron to attend the emperor in his imperial residence. They were relieved every three months. Each of the corps of infantry was on service alternate weeks.

Soon after Bonaparte's elevation to supreme power, he made a grand display in the distribution of the cross of the Legion of Honor to those of his Guard who were selected as members. Surrounded by his magnificent staff, escorted by his troops, met with salvos of cannon, he proceeded to the place where the distribution was to take place. The decorations were taken from a basin of gold, and affixed to each one pronounced worthy of the honor. No one at this day can conceive the excitement and enthusiasm caused by the distribution of this simple decoration. At Boulogne, shortly after, the same distribution was made to the army, and, if possible, in a more imposing manner and causing greater enthusiasm. As Napoleon in the presence of the assembled thousands called the scarred veterans of Italy and Egypt to him and spoke of Montenotte, of Lodi, Arcola, Marengo, of the Pyramids, and of Egypt, tears rolled down their cheeks, and when the cermony was finished, the very heavens rocked to the shouts of "Vive l'Empereur."

In addition to the more regular corps of the Imperial Guard, there was a squadron of Mamelukes, a memento, as it were, of the Pyramids and the battles of the Nile.

It was formed from the corps of "Guides" which Bonaparte had in Egypt, and had nothing of the Mameluke about them but the oriental costume. This squadron with its horse-tail standard, its white heron plumes rising over the Asiatic turban, its timbrels and trumpets and all the trappings of the horses, a la Turk—its elegant dresses covered with gold lace and silk—its bright Damascus blades, presented a most singular yet picturesque appearance, amid the bear skin caps and heavy armor of the cuirassiers. There was also a small corps of Marines, with a blue uniform. It had also two squadrons of gend'armes d'elite, who preformed the police duty at head quarters, and a fine Italian battalion. Its artillery arm was at this time strengthened, numbering in all, 24 pieces of cannon. At the close of the year 1804, the Guard numbered 9,798 men, though nominally composed of but 7000.

CHAPTER 3

Austerlitz & Jena

After a few years of peace, England, by her perfidious violation of the treaty of Amiens, brought on a war between herself and France. Napoleon, no longer shackled by divided power was now free as Caesar. His vast and restless mind could sweep the horizon of his dominions, and find nothing to interfere with his great plans. Laying his hand on the mighty empire, just passed into his keeping, he wielded it with the ease he managed a single army.

With one of the best armies that ever stood on the soil of France, possessing, at the same time, all the advantage of a long rest and thorough discipline, and the experience of veterans, he resolved to punish England for her perfidy, and teach her that while she stirred up Europe to strife and bloodshed, she too might reap the curse of war, carried to her own soil.

But while collecting his vast Flotillas and training his soldiers at Boulogne, preparatory to the invasion of her territory, he was informed that a powerful coalition was forming against him on the Continent. Sweden, Russia, Austria, and England had entered into an alliance, and even Prussia was vacillating between making common cause with the allies and remaining neutral. Called at once from his designs of invading England, the Emperor turned his eye northward, and eastward, and southward, and lo, armies in each direction were marching against him. Four hundred thousand soldiers were making ready to strike France and her territories from four different points. He at once penetrated the designs of the allied soverigns, and with that marvellous power of combination, no other chieftain has ever possessed, he marked out the plan of the entire campaign at Boulogne, predicted the movements of the allied armies, the blunders they would commit, chose his own routes, and accomplished what he proposed. Never had captain, either in ancient or modern times conceived and executed plans on such a scale. "Never indeed had a more mighty mind, possessing greater freedom of will, commanded means more prodigious to operate on such an extent of country." From Calabria to the Gulf of Finland, he had the whole Continent to look after, for he was menaced on every side.

The allies prosecuted their plans leisurely, having little fear of an army encamped on the shores of the ocean. But there was a stir in that camp which portended evil somewhere.

No one knew Napoleon's plans. France even remained in ignorance of them. The army itself was ignorant of its destination, but in twenty days, to the astonishment and consternation of Europe, its terrible standards shook along the Mayn, the Neckar, and the Rhine, and the shout of "Vive l' Empereur," rolled over the plains of Germany. This army Napoleon called the "Grand Army," a name it ever after bore; and those who saw it sweeping on, column after column of infantry, miles of artillery, long files of cavalry, and last of all the Old Guard, with the Emperor in its midst, in all 186,000 men, re-echoed the appellation "The Grand Army."

The Old Guard had left Boulogne by post. Twenty thousand carriages, loaded down with the troops were whirled away towards Germany, whither the army marched with unparalleled speed.

On the 27th of August, most of this immense force lay at Boulogne; on the 25th and 26th of September it crossed the Rhine. On the 13th of October amid a storm of snow, Napoleon harangued the weary troops of Marmont, that had just arrived, and explained to them his plans, and told them he had surrounded the enemy. On the 18th, Mack agreed to surrender Ulm with an army of 80,000 men to him as prisoners of war. By the 20th he could look back on his operations and behold an army of eighty thousand men destroyed, sixty thousand of whom had been taken prisoner with two hundred pieces of cannon, and eighty stands of colors. All this had been done in twenty days, with the loss of less than two thousand men.

On the 13th of November his banners waved over the walls of Vienna. Twelve days after he reconnoitred the field of Austerlitz, and selected it at once as a battle-field where he would overthrow the combined forces of Russia and Austria, led on by their respective soverigns. With 70,000 men he had resolved not to drive back the approaching army of 90,000, but to annihilate it. He refused to take position where he could most effectually check its advance, determined to win all or lose all. Matching his single intellect in the pride of true genius, against the two emperors with their superior army, he cajoled them into a battle when they should have declined it; in order to finish the war with a "clap of thunder."

In the midst of that terrible battle while Soult was ascending the heights of Pratzen, pressing full on the enemy's centre, Lannes thundering on the left with artillery and cavalry, Oudinot on the right re-earning his marshal's staff, Suchet forcing the reluctant enemy before him, a conflict took place in the presence of Napoleon and the allied soverigns which gave a finishing blow to the battle. The Grand Duke Constantine seeing that it was going against

AUSTERLITZ

him, took the whole Russian Imperial Guard and leading them in one dark mass down the heights, moved midway into the low grounds to charge the advancing French. Vandame brought forward his division to meet the shock. While he was thus engaged with this immense and picked body of soldiers, the Grand Duke put himself at the head of two thousand heavy armed cuirassiers of the guards, and burst in resistless strength on the flank of Vandame's division. The French column was rent asunder before it, and three battalions trampled under foot. Napoleon who was advancing to reinforce Soult with the infantry of his guard saw, from a height this overthrow, and exclaimed to Rapp who was by his side, "they are in disorder yonder, that must be set to rights." The latter putting himself at the head of the Mamelukes and chasseurs of the Guard, cried out, "soldiers' you see what has happened below there, they are sabreing our comrades; let us fly to their rescue." Four pieces of horse artillery set off on a gallop in advance. The next moment those fiery horsemen were sweeping with headlong speed upon the Imperial Cavalry. A discharge of grape-shot swept through them thinning them sadly, but not for a moment arresting the charge. The shock was irresistible. Horse and horseman rolled together on the plain. The white heron plumes of the Mamelukes and the shakos of the chasseurs swept like a vision through the overthrown ranks and they were still pressing on even beyond the wreck of their own battalions which had just failed, when the fresh horse guard of Alexander fell upon them. With their horses blown from the severe conflict they had been enduring, this new attack proved too much for them. The brave Morland, Colonel of the Chassuers, was killed on the spot, and the two corps forced back. Napoleon who had watched with the deepest anxiety this terrific meeting of the Imperial Guards, no sooner saw the check of Rapp and the overwhelming force bearing down upon him from the re-formed cuirassiers, than he ordered Bessieres with the horse grenadiers, to charge. Not a moment was to be lost, the bugles rang forth the charge, and like a single man that living mass of disciplined valor went pouring forward to the strife. The steady gallop of their heavy horses shook the plain, and so accurate and regular was their swift movement, that they appeared like a dark and ponderous wave rolling onward. But the crest it bore was composed of glittering steel. Right gallantly was that tremendous onset received, and those vast bodies of cavalry the elite of both armies became mixed in a hand to hand fight. The firing of the infantry ceased, for the shot told on friend and foe alike. The soldiers rested on their arms and gazed with astonishment on that rearing, plunging mass from which was heard naught but fierce shouts and ringing steel as blade crossed blade in the fierce collision. The emperors of Russia and Germany on one height and Napoleon on another, watched with indescribable anxiety this strange encounter between the flower of their troops. At length the Imperial Guard of the enemy gave way. The bugles of the Old Guard then rang cheerily out, and Vandame charging anew, infantry and cavalry were driven in disorder almost to the walls of Austerlitz. Their artillery and standards fell into the hands of the victors. Napoleon's joy was extreme on beholding this triumph of his Guard over that of the Russian emperor.

The two soverigns had tried their last and heaviest blow, and had failed, and the battle though unended, was already won. Napoleon had not merely defeated, he had routed and nearly annihilated the combined armies, and the two emperors were fugitives on the field. This wonderful mind had thus in a few months ended the war. Never did his genius shine out in greater brilliancy. "The secrecy and rapidity of the march of so vast a body of troops across France; the semicircular process by which they interposed between Mack and the hereditary states and compelled the surrender of that unhappy chief with half his army; the precision with which nearly two hundred thousand men converging from the shores of the channel, the coasts of Brest, the marshes of Holland, and the banks of the Elbe were made to arrive each at the hour appointed around the ramparts of Ulm, the swift advance on Vienna; the subsequent fan-like dispersion of the army to overawe the hereditary states their sudden concentration for the decisive fight at Austerlitz; the skill displayed in that contest itself and the admirable account to which he turned the fatal cross march of the allied soverigns, are so many proofs of military ability never exceeded even in the annals of his previous triumphs."

It is not to be supposed that in this great battle the action of the Imperial Guard was confined to a cavalry charge. Napoleon found himself so inferior in numerical force, that he did not husband the Guard, as he afterwards did in Russia. He divided it up among different corps of the army, where they furnished an example during all that bloody day to the other troops, which made them irresistible. Pressing side by side with those bear-skin caps, they knew no repulse. In the previous battles the Guard had taken little part, and murmured grievously at their idleness, but at Austerlitz they were led into the thickest of the fight. Soult had under him ten battalions of the Guard. Oudinot and Davoust had ten battalions of the Grenadiers, and wild work did they make under those chieftains, with the stubborn ranks of the enemy. Their artillery was served throughout the battle, with terrible rapidity and precision. Forty guns were at the disposal of the Guard, and wherever immediate help was wanted, thither they were hurried, sending desolation through the hostile ranks.

At the commencement of the battle, Napoleon retained near him only the Cavalry of the Guard, the mounted Chasseurs, the Grenadiers and Mamelukes. These were for a reserve, and were massed together, ranged in two lines, and by squadrons, and under the command of Bessieres and Rapp. Its light artillery, however, did fearful execution. It was every where belching forth fire. It was one of its batteries that played upon the frozen lake over which a column was endeavoring to pass, and breaking the ice with its shot, sank two thousand in the water. It deployed with such rapidity, that is movements appeared more like cavalry in motion, than artillery, and the soldiers jokingly called it "Hussars on wheels."

THE OLD GUARD AT JENA

These overwhelming victories made the allies desirous of peace, which was soon after ratified at Presbourg. But in the final settlement of the vexed questions of territory, Prussia felt herself so aggrieved and humbled, that she rashly flew into arms before the French army had all left Germany. An immense force was assembled, and she, single-handed, resolved to overthrow the Conqueror of Europe, and that too with the army of the latter not yet beyond the Rhine. Napoleon beheld with sorrow this new war thrown upon his hands just as he had finished an arduous campaign and completed a peace, and was at first depressed. He saw only new dangers arise, as old ones were removed. But in the excitement of preparation these gloomy thoughts disappeared, and he rapidly made ready to meet the evils that threatened him. The Old Guard was immediately ordered to return. Transported in carriages, of which there were relays the whole route, they moved with the speed of Cavalry, and in a few days were again beyond the Rhine. A hundred and eighty thousand Germans composed the army of Prussia. Napoleon had a larger force under him, to say nothing of the vast makeweight of his genius against the imbecility of his adversary.

The battle of Jena, fought on the same day as that of Auerstadt, under Davoust, finished the Prussian king. At Jena, Napoleon had before him a force inferior to his own, although he supposed the whole Prussian army was on the heights of Landgrafenberg. Up the steep ascent that led to this plateau, already occupied by the enemy, he resolved to head his army. At first the corps of Lannes and the Old Guard climbed through the ravines to the top. The Guard, four thousand strong, were then ordered to encamp in a square, and in the centre Napoleon pitched his tent. A pile of stones to this day marks the spot where he bivouacked, and the people of the vicinity have changed the name of the height into Napoleons berg. It was found such a heavy task to drag the artillery up the precipitous sides of the mountain, that search was made for an easier ascent. A ravine was discovered, but on examination it proved too narrow to admit the carriages. A detachment of engineers was immediately sent to cut away the rick, while to cheer on the men, wearied with their day's march, Napoleon himself held a torch for them to work by. Late at night he ascended the heights and passed into the squares of the Old Guard, to snatch a few hours repose. But as he approached their dark and motionless ranks around which only a few fires were kindled, he cast his eyes over the plateau and saw the fires of the enemy covering its entire extent and farther away to the right with the old castle of Echartsberg above them, those of the Duke of Brunswick.

In the morning before daylight, he was up and the soldiers stood to arms. It was cold and chilly and a fog enveloped the heights. Escorted by torches which shed a lurid light on his staff and on the ranks, he went along their front haranguing the soldiers, bidding them receive the Prussian cavalry with firmness, and promising a glorious victory. The shout "forward" which followed, was borne to the enemy's camp.

The Old Guard, as usual, was ordered up to close the battle. As it advanced the whole line threw itself impetuously forward, and the field became covered with fugitives. Out of the 70,000 who had entered the battle, "not a corps remained entire."

Advancing rapidly, the Grand Army entered Berlin on the 28th. For the first time, Napoleon made a triumphal entry into a conquered capital. Surrounded by the Old Guard dressed in rich uniform, he passed through the city. The dismounted chasseurs and grenadiers were in front, the horse grenadiers and chasseurs in the rear—in the middle rode Berthier, Duroc, Davoust, and Augereau, while in the centre of the last group in an open space by himself, rode Napoleon. He, and that Old Guard enfolding him in triumph as it had done in danger, were the centre of all eyes.

In a month he had overturned the Prussian monarchy and destroyed its boasted armies—the soldiers of the great Frederic. The overthrow of an empire was no longer the work of years, Napoleon dispatched it in a few weeks.

Several changes had passed over the Old Guard during the last two years. Augmented as it had been, the expense of keeping it up was found to be too great. Neither would the mode of recruiting it by drawing the best troops from the line answer in a long and destructive war. It took away too many good soldiers and tended to demoralize the army. There had been previously created a corps of velites, a sort of enlisted volunteers to remedy the last evil by drawing from them instead of the army. But this also was too expensive, and Napoleon therefore formed a new regiment called the "fusilliers of the Guard," the soldiers of which should be selected from the annual contingent, the officers alone to be taken from the Guard.

The velites were required to be young men of family. This was to obtain a certain amount of education and character, with which is usually joined a sense of honor, so important in a corps. Allured by the splendid renown of this new conqueror, dazzled by his amazing victories, young aspirants for fame flocked to his standard. Among them were many very young men. One of these, an only son of one of the most opulent families of the province in which he lived, enlisted at the age of eighteen. Very fair and delicate, he appeared much younger, yet he cheerfully endured the fatigues of the march, and stood firm under the fire of the enemy. After the fall of Berlin, this young velite marched with the army into Varsovie and nobly endured the hardships of the dreadful winter campaign that followed.

It was Napoleon's custom in campaign to halt in the open country to take his meals. On these occasions he always had a dozen or so velites or chasseurs in a circle close around his person, to prevent any one from approaching. One day during a halt, as his faithful Mameluke, Roustan, was preparing his coffee, he saw a boyish velite posted opposite him. Struck by his beauty and aristocratic air, he called him and abruptly asked, "Who put you in my Guard?"

"Your majesty," replied the young Desherbiers.

"I do not understand you," said Napoleon, "explain yourself."

"Sire, after the decree of your majesty which permitted young men of family to serve in your Guard, I fulfilled the required conditions, and am at my post."

"Thou are a little fellow," said the Emperor, chuckling him under the chin.

"Sire, I perform my duties the same as the largest in the regiment."

"Have you ever been under fire?"

"Yes, Sire, at the passage of Berg."

"That was warm work. Were you not a little afraid. Ah, ah, you blush, I have hit the truth."

"Yes, Sire, I own it, but it lasted only a moment."

"Never mind, many others like thee have been afraid and it lasted a much longer time." After a short silence, he resumed, "thou are a good young man and like the rest of us, thou hast paid the tribute. Thou shalt dine with me, will that please thee?"

"Certainly, Sire!" cried the young velite, while his eyes sparkled with joy at the honor shown him, and placing his carbine near him he sat down opposite the emperor. Roustan waited on him with all the deference he would have shown to a general officer. Desherbiers took the slice of bacon which was handed him on a silver plate and began to eat with the voracious appetite his short allowance and hard duties had given him. As the Mameluke turned the wine into a silver goblet, Napoleon said smiling, "Ah, ah, garcon, thou likest well to be served in a goblet, so that one cannot see how much thou drinkest. I wager that thou hast it refilled."

"Even to the brim, Sire, the better to drink to the health of your Majesty."

Napoleon joked him incessantly during the repast, but the young velite's replies were full of spirit and point. After it was over, he asked him his name, "Guiyot Desherbiers, Sire," he replied. Repeating the name over after him, he asked him if he was relative to a counsellor by that name in Paris, not long since dead. Being answered in the negative, he added, "very well, conduct yourself properly and I will see to your advancement when the proper time shall come."

The young velite made his military salute, took his carbine and was again at his post.

JENA

I have related this anecdote to show on what terms Napoleon was with his guard, and also the means he took to bind the brave to him. In the spirit and nonchalance of this young velite, his military ambition and education, he saw at a glance a future officer—one of those granite pillars like Lannes, Ney, Massena, Davoust, and others who were carrying his victorious eagles over Europe.

After his return from his campaign, Napoleon went one day to see the velite, who, having been separated from the chasseurs, were stationed at Versailles. As he approached the squadron, he requested the commander to order young Desherbiers from the ranks. The officer replied that he had been passed into a regiment of hussars, and was not in Spain.

"Why was he put there, he was but in infant?"

"On account of his gallant conduct at Friedland. He slew two Russian grenadiers with his own hand in sight of the whole squadron."

"That makes a difference," said Napoleon, "it is all well."

The young velite, however, never returned, he was taken by guerrillas, who put him to death with the most cruel tortures. He bore all with heroic courage, and with his last breath pronounced the names of Napoleon and a fair cousin in Paris.

This incident illustrates forcibly the remarkable memory of Napoleon. The terrible scenes through which he had passed, the world of care that lay on his shoulders— plunged as he was into the very vortex of European politics and engaged with designs vast as a hemisphere—did not make him forget the young velite who had dined with him in Poland. This memory of the commonest soldier if he had shown any remarkable traits, or performed any deeds of valor had a wonderful effect on the troops. Each one felt that he was directly under the eyes of his sovereign and commander. He saw and remembered all that was done, and skill and daring would not go unrewarded. Slight as it may seem, next to the veneration his genius and deeds inspired, this was the great secret of the strange power he had over his troops.

The chasseurs always surrounded Napoleon's person during a campaign. It was necessary they should be ready at a moment's warning, for the movements of this ubiquitous being were sudden as lightning. When starting for the army he generally departed from St. Cloud, in the middle of the night or at one or two o'clock in the morning, and sometimes made two hundred and fifty miles in twenty-four hours. Often he would stop for several hours, to dictate despatches, but at the words "allots, the carriage, to horse, gentlemen," there was "mounting in hot haste," and away they dashed, in a headlong gallop. An aid-de-camp was always stationed on horseback at the left side of the door of the carriage and an ecuyer at the right—the officers of ordinance, pages, piqueurs holding the horses by the head. Roustan, the Mameluke, and the domestics followed close after the carriage. Twenty-four mounted chasseurs of the Guard completed the cortege, which swept like a tempest along the road. In this manner he would go twenty, thirty, and sometimes nearly forty miles without halting. When he stopped all flung themselves from their horses at once, except the chasseurs, who remained in the saddle. But if he left the carriage, half of them immediately dismounted, and fixing their bayonets to their carbines presented arms, and stood facing outward, around him. But none of the officers left their places unless he permitted it. When he wished to observe the enemy through his glass, the number of the Guard was doubled and formed in a square about him. This square adapted itself to his movements, enlarging or contracting itself, but never coming nearer than twenty-five or thirty steps to his person.

When he distributed favors to his Guard, such as grades, titles, or decorations, unless it was immediately after a victory, every one knew that some serious affair was at hand. The review of the regiments of the Guard recently arrived, or harangues to his troops, was a certain prelude to an approaching battle. These harangues always produced a magical effect; but nothing perhaps excited so wild enthusiasm as the presentation of the eagle to a new regiment of the Guard. On the day of the ceremony, the regiment with its arms and uniforms in perfect order, marched to the place appointed and formed into three close columns, the three fronts turning towards the centre—the space for the fourth being reserved for the superior officers and the suite of the emperor. As soon as the latter appeared, the officers put themselves in advance in a single rank, so that he approached alone. By the simplicity of his dress he became more conspicuous, and presented a striking contract to the brilliant uniforms of his officers, which were sprinkled over with decorations and embroidered with silver and gold. After receiving the orders of the emperor, the prince of Wagram, in his office of major-general, dismounted, and caused the colors to be taken from their case and unfolded before the troops. The drums then beat the march, and Berthier advancing, took the eagle from the hands of the officer and approached several steps toward Napoleon. The latter uncovering himself saluted the banner; and removing the glove from his right hand, lifted it towards the eagle and in a solemn and distinct voice said:

"Soldiers, I confide to you the French eagle; I commit it to your valor and patriotism. It will be your guide and rallying pivot. You swear never to abandon it. You swear to prefer death to the dishonor of seeing it torn from your hands. You swear it?"

The last words were pronounced with sudden energy, and in a moment the swords of the officers shook in the air, and "Yes, yes we swear it," rolled in one prolonged shout along the lines. The bands of music then struck in and "Vive l' Empereur," was repeated in frenzied accents over the field.

In 1806, the Guard was composed of 15,656 men.

CHAPTER 4
Eylau

The utter overthrow of the Prussian armies at Jena and Auerstadt did not wring a peace from the king. Russia had formed an alliance with him, and her troops were already on the march for the frontiers of his kingdom. To meet this new enemy, Napoleon pushed on into Poland, where he designed to take up his winter quarters. This unhappy country received him with open arms, hoping, through his instrumentality, once more to have a national existence. At the outset a Polish guard of honor was formed, which, together with the squadron of the Imperial Guard, was to look to the security of the emperor's person. Its fidelity and zeal suggested to Napoleon the idea of incorporating into the Old Guard a corps of light cavalry, composed entirely of Poles. A decree to that effect was issued, and four squadrons of lancers were joined to the cavalry.

PAINFUL MARCH OF THE IMPERIAL GUARD
BEFORE THE BATTLE OF EYLAU

Before the winter set in there was a short campaign, in which the Russians were forced to retire, but the roads were in such a horrible state that the pursuit was slow and painful. The cavalry horses sunk up to their knees, and could only move on a walk. The artillery stuck in the mud and snow, and would not be pushed forward. Napoleon put forth prodigious efforts with the Old Guard, to strike a decisive blow. These veterans, covered with sleet and snow, waded knee deep through the mud, performing the most painful marches with cheerfulness, because their leader was in their midst. Alternate snow, freezing weather, and thaws, exhausted their strength and benumbed their limbs. Their bivouacs at night were either on frozen ground or in fields made soft by the melted snow.

The pursuit ended at Naiselle, which the enemy suddenly evacuated. Napoleon entered a cabin to pass the night, and as one was cleaning out the straw, he uncovered a corpse which some faithful hand had concealed. The next day he began to retrace his steps to Varsovie, and took up his winter quarters.

The two armies remained inactive till near the close of December, when the Russian general resolved to surprise Napoleon by a winter march; and, cutting his line in two, separate the two wings. The latter, penetrating his design concentrated his troops and advanced to give him battle. They met at Eylau.

I shall not attempt a new description of this great butchery, in which the conquerors gained but a barren victory. The Old Guard at the commencement was placed in the cemetery of Eylau, into which the enemy's balls were soon crashing with murderous effect.

The attack of Augereau, and the terrible overthrow of his division, brought on one of those crises which compelled Napoleon to launch his grand reserve, the Old Guard, upon the enemy. Nothing could have been farther from his wishes than to compromise his reserve so early in the battle. But the danger was imminent. A column of Russian grenadiers following up the flight of Augereau had penetrated into the cemetery where Napoleon stood, surrounded only by a hundred of his personal guard. Hour after hour he had stood unmoved while the cannon balls were crashing on the steeple and walls of the church above him. Without changing a feature he had seen the annihilation of Augereau's division, and now with equal composure beheld three or four thousand grenadiers almost at his feet. Ordering his personal Guard to advance and check them, he called up a battalion of the foot-guard a little in the rear. There were six battalions that had taken no part in the contest except to stand and see their ranks rent by shot. With joy, therefore, they saw a prospect of mingling in the strife. Two battalions disputed the honor of charging the Russians. The first in order marched forward, and without stopping to fire, overthrew the victorious grenadiers with the bayonet.

In the meantime the terrible cavalry charge of Murat was preparing. Seventy squadrons, or more than fourteen thousand horse, in all the splendor of battle array, swept full on the Russian centre, stormed over their batteries and breaking the first line of infantry pushed on to the second, driving it back to the wood, where a battery of heavy artillery at last checked their victorious advance. In the meantime the broken first line rallied and began to hem in Murat. It was then that General Lepee, a brave and heroic officer, was ordered to charge with the horse grenadiers of the Guard. The heavy and iron clad squadrons galloped, shouting to the rescue of their comrades. Riding through the groups of infantry that had rallied, they smote down everything in their passage. The close fire of the artillery and charges of infantry made horrible gaps in their ranks, and around them shook as wild and disordered a field as the wintry heavens ever looked upon, but nothing could arrest their strong gallop. Compact as iron—and as the thunder cloud when rent by the lightning closes swiftly again, so did those stern squadrons close over every rent made by the destructive batteries, and in one black mass crossed and recrossed the field in every direction. Through the driving snow occasional glimpses of it was got by Napoleon, and with joy he saw it unbroken sweep the field in the face of the enemy.

Murat was relieved and able to re-form his cavalry and bring it off in good order, while the Russian centre was dreadfully shattered. General Dohlman, commander of the mounted chasseurs of the Guard, fell not fifteen steps from the Russian line. One of the chasseurs seeing his general under the bayonets of the enemy spurred recklessly forward in the fire, and dismounting, lifted him upon his horse. Surrounded by Russian hussars, he in turn received several wounds, one of which dislocated his arm. He was about to fall overpowered by numbers, when one of his comrades, a chasseur of his squadron, seeing his peril fought his way up to him and relieved him. By the boldness of these two chasseurs, their general was enabled to get near the French lines before he died, and was thus spared the mortification of seeing himself a prisoner of the enemy. All the officers and soldiers of the Guard on this murderous day sustained the reputation gained in a hundred battles, and Napoleon loaded it with eulogiums. A Lieutenant Morlay, a color bearer of the 1st battalion of the 1st regiment of foot grenadiers, had the staff of his colors broken above and below his hand by the bursting of a shell which killed an officer and wounded five of his guard. But instead of showing surprise, he coolly took up the colors and fixing the staff to a musket, carried them into the battle. A captain of the mounted grenadiers of the Guard, mortally wounded lay extended on the snow, when some of his comrades coming up, wished to remove him. "Leave me alone, my friends," he said, "I am content since we have the victory, and I die on the field of battle."

JENA

We will pass over the heart-rending scene the snow-covered field presented next morning. Napoleon had never in his bloody career beheld such a spectacle, and he was more unnerved than in the most perilous crisis of the battle. One of his generals seeing his agitation, endeavored to lessen the evil by saying it was exaggerated, and spoke of the new glory the victory would give him. "To a father," replied Napoleon, "who loses his children, victory has no charms—when the heart speaks glory itself is an illusion." The enemies of Bonaparte receive such manifestations of feeling on his part, with a smile of incredulity, declaring it impossible that a man whose whole career was marked with blood, and to whom the desolation and horrors of a battle- field were accustomed spectacles, could ever utter such a sentiment in sincerity. To other military chieftains they award all the kindly and noble feelings belonging to men in civic life. The scenes of slaughter through which they pass do not make wild beasts of them. The English generals in carrying out the aggressive policy of their government, and Russian and Austrian commanders are endowed with the feelings common to our race, and yet the terrible battle which had heaped the snow plains of Eylau with dead bodies was fought in a defensive war on the part of Napoleon. Prussia declared war against him, and Russia without the shadow of a reason, became her ally, and yet how few in this country ever think of blaming the real criminals in the affair, but on the contrary, heap on Napoleon the sin of it all.

But independent of this, such a sentiment was natural to any man, even the most abandoned of our race. No wretch is so hardened as not to love even the beast that has carried him faithfully and nobly through imminent perils, or the dog which has watched and defended him. Much less could a commander like Napoleon look on the bloody ranks, stiff in death, that had stood like walls of iron around him the day before, without a heart full of grief. His brave Guard too, that carried him in its arms, and which would not see him taken while a single man remained alive to strike a blow for him, had left its dead everywhere. He had lost his defenders, those who cherished him in their hearts while living, and murmured his name in dying, and he felt like one robbed of his treasures that he had hoarded with so much care—of valiant hearts that beat but for him. It required a heart of stone to look on those gallant men, mangled and torn, and heaped in thousands over the blood-stained snow and not be profoundly moved. Napoleon was overcome by it. The excitement of the battle was over, the victory won, and the feelings of our common nature triumphed over the stern will of the chieftain and the pride of the conqueror. He could not conceal his emotion, it exhibited itself even in his bulletin.

The white uniform had been introduced into many of the regiments, but the contrast it presented to the blood stains of those who wore it, so shocked him that he immediately ordered it to be lain aside by the survivors, and blue to used instead, cost what it might. He rode over the field to look after the wounded, and sent out all his domestics to relieve them, while the chasseurs of the Guard took their horses and helped bring them into camp.

The rest of the winter and spring passed in quietness, but in the beginning of June hostilities recommenced, and Napoleon started in pursuit of the enemy. At the bloody battles of Heilsberg, the Young Guard astonished the army by its intrepidity and desperate courage. The battle of Friedland followed, and the allied armies were rolled into the Alle. Napoleon spared his Guard in this battle and at night bivouacked on the field amid its squares. The soldiers were angry that they had not been allowed to take part in the victory, and one of its intrepid leaders said, "the Guard was treated like beasts in being compelled to remain with their arms crossed all day."

If Napoleon had shown himself a great general in this campaign, he exhibited no less the skillful diplomatist in bringing about a peace. He first met Alexander on a raft moored in the middle of the Niemen, while the opposing banks were lined with the hostile armies, which no sooner saw the two emperors embrace, than they rent the air with shouts. In a few days Alexander was established in Napoleon's household and ate at his table. The poor king of Prussia was neglected and humbled. The two monarchs rode together and sat hour after hour in private tete-a-tete, until Alexander became completely fascinated. He reviewed the Old Guard with Napoleon, and was struck with their martial bearing and perfect discipline, and lavished on them high enconiums. The Guard in return shouted, "Vive Alexander, Vive Napoleon."

Days passed away in this social intercourse and each succeeding one found the Russian monarch more and more captivated. On returning from these interviews he would exclaim, "What a great man, what a genius, what extensive views, what a captain, what a statesman! Had I but known him sooner how many faults he might have spared me, what great things we might have accomplished together." Alexander was ambitious, and Napoleon knew it. He therefore opened to him plans of empire, pointed where new realms and glory could be won, and sketched plans so vast and yet so feasible, that the young emperor seemed to have opened his eyes on a new world. Napoleon convinced him that alliance with England and Austria was ruinous, while should they two combine, they could dictate terms to half the world. The clear and masterly manner in which he sketched the perfidious policy of his foes, the generous offers he made to him a conquered enemy, and the vast sphere he pointed out to the young aspirant after glory soon brought about the end he was after. A treaty was made with Prussia which stripped that unfortunate monarch of a large part of his kingdom. Another treaty was concluded with Russia. Lastly, a secret treaty or alliance offensive and defensive, not to be published till both consented to it, was signed, by which the two monarchs were to make common cause, by sea and land, and to declare war against England if she would not subscribe to the conditions of the two open treaties. This was the famous peace of Tilsit.

In 1807 the Guard counted 15,361 men.

On the conquest of Spain, in 1808, the Imperial Guard was rarely called into action. It however performed some extraordinary marches. In a rash attack by Lefebvre Desnouettes with the chasseurs of the Guard, some sixty of the latter were taken prisoners, which annoyed Napoleon much. They were his favorite troops, and he could not bear to have them in the hands of the enemy. He always wore their uniform in battle, and at St. Helena, when about to die, he put it on, and was laid in state in it after his death.

While prosecuting his march from Benavente, pressing eagerly after the English, a courier arrived from Paris bringing news of the union of Austria to the European confederacy against him, and the mustering of her armies. On receiving the courier's package, he ordered a bivouac fire to be kindled, and sitting down, was soon lost in thought, while the snow fell thick and fast about him. His plans were instantly taken. On the spot he wrote an order for the raising of 80,000 conscripts in France. He then proceeded thoughtfully to Astorga, where he remained two days, writing despatches. Every hour was occupied, his secretaries were put on one of those strains he in great emergencies demanded. Momentous affairs claimed his attention. His armies in Spain, France, and all Europe, lay like a map in his mighty mind, and he grasped the whole. To the different divisions of his army in Spain he sent despatches to guide their conduct, he sketched the course to be followed in pursuing the English, issued directions for regulating the internal affairs of the kingdom, and organized his plan for the overthrow of the coalition against him. He stopped five days longer at Valladolid, employed in writing despatches to every part of Europe. In these five days he accomplished the work of a year, and having finished all, he mounted his horse and posted like a flash of lightning for Paris. In the first five hours he rode the astonishing distance of eighty-five miles, or seventeen miles an hour. He then took carriage while the Imperial Guard marched swiftly towards Germany to meet the army he was to concentrate there. This wild gallop of eighty-five miles was long remembered by the inhabitants of the towns through which the smoking cavalcade of the emperor passed. Relays of horses had been provided along the road, and no sooner did he arrive at one post then he flung himself on a fresh horse, and sinking the spurs in his flanks, dashed away in headlong speed. Few who saw that short figure surmounted with a plain chapeau, sweep by on that day, ever forgot it. His pale face was calm as marble, but his lips were compressed and his brow knit like iron, while his flashing eye as he leaned forward, still jerking impatiently at the bridle as if to accelerate his speed, seemed to devour the distance. No one spoke, but the whole suite strained forward in the breathless race. The gallant chasseurs never had had so long and wild a ride before.

It is not probable that Napoleon kept up this locomotive speed for eighty-five miles in order to gain two or three hours of time. No battle was pending which an hour's delay might los; and whether he reached Paris at five o'clock or eight, could make no difference in his plans. The truth is, it was the only outlet he had to his stormy feelings. While occupied with his army in Spain, he had been suddenly told that a fearful coalition was arming against him in the north of Europe. Colossus as he was, he could not but be painfully excited at the magnitude of the dangers that threatened him. He saw the motive which prompted this sudden blow and felt that it might prove decisive. He could not take his veteran troops on which he relied, from Spain, and he must raise a new army. The seven days he spent in writing despatches, after the arrival of the courier from Paris, were seven days of such mental labor as ordinary men never dream of. In that time he performed the work of a year to most men. The vast field over which his mind labored, the complicated and vital affairs that claimed his attention, the thousand objects, each of which was sufficient to task the strongest mind, taken up and disposed of in these few days, and the plan of a great campaign marked out for himself, caused a mental strain that brought his physical system, firm and iron-like as it was, into such a state of nervous excitement, that this fierce ride relieved him. Physical exhaustion was medicine to him for it took the fire from his brain.

CHAPTER 5

The Young Guard

Austria as we have seen, with a perfidy that belongs to her national character, no sooner found Napoleon involved in the Spanish war, and the elite of his army there, than she resolved to violate her sacred treaty and drive the French troops that still remained in Germany, over the Rhine. The court thought to take its hated foe unawares, and so it had, forgetting the celerity of his movements and the rapid development of his plans.

No sooner had he arrived in Paris, than he despatched Berthier to Germany to take charge of and concentrate his troops that were scattered from the Alps to the Baltic. In the meantime he organized eight new regiments to augment the infantry of his guard, two of tirailleurs grenadiers, two of tirailleurs chasseurs, and two of conscript chasseurs, in all 6000 men.

These were called the Young Guard, although incorporated with the Old. Together they formed an imposing body of troops. On almost every breast of the Old Guard glittered the star of the Legion of Honor, won by bravery on the field of battle.

Every thing being ready the troops were sent by forced marches to the Rhine. On the 12th of April, Napoleon set out from St. Cloud, and in six days arrived at head-quarters. It was high time he had come, for Berthier had done nothing but commit blunders, and but for the tardiness of the allies, the French army would have been driven across the Rhine before his arrival. It was scattered over forty leagues—in forty-eight hours it was concentrated in the space of ten leagues and ready to deliver its terrible blows. The continental armies opposed to Napoleon have been much blamed for their slow and cautious advances, when the position of the French army was such that by celerity of movement they could have inflicted heavy disasters upon it. But military critics forget that Napoleon's tactics completely baffled the oldest generals of the continent. Nine tenths of the time their combinations were broken up before the battle took place. This wizard, by his rapid movements, audacious advances, and bold and daring attacks, so confused them, that they never knew when he was strong or weak. They were afraid to compromise their forces by any bold push, for whenever they did, he came thundering on their flanks. No wonder they became careful, for if they attempted a surprise or skilful manœuvre as at Austerlitz, they found it was just what their imperial foe desired. In fact, such was his eagle glance and far-reaching intellect, that it was impossible for the Austrians or Prussians to attempt a manœuvre in his presence without getting his victorious squadrons on their flanks. They had so often suffered from these flank attacks, that the precautions they took to avoid them were frequently ludicrous, and crippled all their actions.

The Emperor arrived on the night of the 17th—on the 19th the battle of Abensberg was fought which broke the enemy's centre—the 21st, he attacked the enemy at Landshut, and put him to flight. On the 22d he was victorious at Echmuhl, and pushed the Austrians over the Danube, which they had to cross under the tremendous fire of the batteries of the Old Guard.

RATISBON

On the 23d, Ratisbon was carried by assault and the enemy forced to make a rapid retreat. One hundred pieces of cannon, forty standards, fifty thousand prisoners, three thousand baggage wagons, were the extraordinary fruits of these five days' labor. It required, however, a constitution of iron to stand the strain he put on himself at this time. Riding six days in succession to reach the army, he immediately set to work concentrating it, and preparing for battle. It is said that the letters to his officers during the next five days would have made a volume. He was on horseback or dictating letters eighteen hours out of every twenty-four during the whole time. He outstripped his own saddle horses sent on as relays, and broke down those of the king of Bavaria, his ally, and yet when his staff and assistants were completely knocked up, he would sit calmly down and dictate despatches half the night. He seemed every where during these five days, and his blows fell with the rapidity and power of thunderbolts.

After the taking of Ratisbon he issued a proclamation to his troops in which after recounting their victories he promised in one month to bring them under the walls of Vienna. In just one month he was there, although to accomplish it he had to wade through the terrible slaughter of Ebersberg.

He was at Landshut the 26th of April, where he found the Old Guard which had just arrived from Spain. In the beginning of January it was at Astorga at the foot of the Gallician mountains—on the 26th of April it was in the heart of the Austrian empire, having performed one of the most extraordinary marches on record. Napoleon's eye flashed with delight when he saw once more his favorite corps of old veterans, twenty thousand strong, fresh from the battle-fields of Spain, defile before him. The Guard was no less delighted to see its chieftain, and rent the air with shouts of "Vive l' Empereur."

Arriving before Vienna, he placed his batteries, and in ten hours threw ten thousand shells into the city. The crash of falling dwellings, the bursting of shells, and the ascending flames streaking the heavens in every quarter, made the night of May 12th one long to be remembered by the Viennese.

At this time the young princess, Maria Louisa, the future bride of the Emperor, lay sick in the imperial palace, and unable to be removed. This being communicated to Napoleon, he ordered the direction of the batteries to be changed; and thus amid general devastation and death, she remained unharmed. This was the first introduction of himself to the princess, and it must be confessed it was wild and stern enough. "It was by the thunders of artillery and the flaming light of bombs across tile sky, that his first addresses were made, the first accents of tenderness were from the deep booming of mortars which but for his interposition would have consigned her father's palace to destruction."

Vienna fell, and Napoleon with a part of his Guard took up his quarters at Schoenbrun.

While here an incident occurred which showed with what severity the least license on the part of his Old Guard was visited. One of its chief surgeons was lodged in the suburbs of the city, at the house of an aged canoness, and near relative of Prince Lichtenstein.

One day having taken too much wine, he wrote her an extravagant and impertinent letter in which he introduced the name of Lefebvre in a disgraceful manner. She immediately threw herself on the protection of General Andreossy, whom Napoleon had made governor of the city, and to whom she sent the letter she had received. The governor forwarded both her letter and the surgeon's to the emperor. The latter immediately sent an order for the surgeon to appear on parade the following morning. The next morning as Napoleon descended rapidly the steps of the palace his countenance betokened an explosion at hand, and without speaking to any one, he advanced towards the ranks holding the letters in his hand, and called out, "Let M—— —— advance." The surgeon approached, when the emperor extending the letter towards him said, "Did you write this infamous letter?"

"Pardon sire," cried the overwhelmed surgeon, "I was drunk at the time, and did not know what I did."

"Miserable man, to outrage one of my brave lieutenants and at the same time a canoness worthy of respect, and sufficiently bowed down with the miseries of war. I do not admit your excuse. I degrade you from the Legion of Honor, you are unworthy to bear that venerated symbol. General Dorsenne," said he, addressing the chief of the corps, "see that this order is executed. Insult an aged woman! I respect an aged woman as if she were my mother."

The poor surgeon was a peaceable man, upright in his conduct when sober, and esteemed in the Guard as much for his kindness as for his talents. They interceded for him, but Napoleon refused to grant their petition, nor did he yield until a paper signed by all the generals of the Guard, asking his pardon was presented. Excesses are always committed by a victorious army, but the inhabitants of a city conquered by the French never complained of the conduct of the Old Guard. At home and abroad they were the friends of the citizen and exhibited an uprightness of character rarely found in any body of troops.

Leaving Vienna, Napoleon crossed the Danube at Lobau, and concentrated the whole Austrian army on the opposite side. The sudden rise of the river after part of the army had crossed by which the bridges were swept away leaving him with only a portion of his troops and artillery, the bloody battle of Aspern, the failure of ammunition, the defeat of the French, and the death of Lannes are well known. Napoleon was compelled to use his Guard severely on both of these days to check the victorious advance of the enemy. Bessieres closed the first day's battle with one of those splendid charges of the cavalry of the Guard on the Austrians' centre. Riding up to the flaming batteries, he forced them back into the squares of the infantry. The reserve cavalry of the Austrians were sent against them, but were swept from their path like chaff, and with clattering armor and deafening shouts, the terrible squadrons threw themselves on the solid Hungarian squares and rode round and round them in search of an opening through which they could dash, till nearly half their number was stretched on the plain, and they were compelled to retire.

The next day after various successes on either side, the battle at length turned decidedly in favor of the Austrians. Night was approaching, and as a last resort, Napoleon ordered Lannes to pierce the Austrian centre. His terrible columns had well nigh succeeded, when the ammunition gave way. Stopped in his victorious advance, he at length was compelled to retrace his steps and the whole army was ordered to fall back towards the island of Lobau. Seeing the retrograde movement the Archduke John pushed his attack with greater vigor and under the tremendous fire of his eighty guns the French soon began to show signs of disorder. It was all important at this crisis that the village of Essling should still be held, for if taken by the enemy Napoleon saw that his case would be desperate. The Archduke John also perceived the vital importance of this post, for it would effectually cut off the retreat of the French to the river; and sent a tremendous force against it which drove out its gallant defenders from every portion but the great granary. Napoleon calm and unmoved, resolved at once to retake it, cost what it might? and for that purpose immediately despatched a portion

Aspern Essling

of the Old Guard—his never failing hope when every-thing else gave way. The drums beat a hurried charge, and the dark column, in double quick time, moved over the interval, and with fixed bayonets and firm front entered the village. No shouts or clatter of small arms herald-ed their approach or marked their terrible course. With the unwavering strength of the inrolling tide of the sea, they swept forward, crushing every obstacle in their pas-sage. Through the devouring fire, over the batteries, they stormed on, and pushing steadily against the dark and overwhelming masses that opposed their progress, they rolled the two Austrian columns in affright and dismay before them. They knew the mission they were to fulfil, and ten times their number could not have resisted their heavy onset. No sudden alarms, no thoughts of retreat, no anxiety weakened their high purpose. The crash of cannon balls in their midst, the headlong charge of cav-alry, could not disturb their firm set ranks. They moved resistlessly forward till the enemy was driven out of the village, and then they established themselves in the gra-nary, from which the most determined efforts were made to dislodge them. The Hungarian grenadiers, that had stood so firm before the onset of Lannes' columns, were sent against them, but were hurled back in confusion. Again did they return with reinforcements, and pressed up to the very foot of the walls and again fed before the murderous fire that met them. Five times did they return with desperate courage to the assault, only to meet the same fate. The upper part of the building took fire in the tumult, but still "amid the roar of burning timbers" and incessant rattle of musketry the Old Guard fought on. The Austrian general seeing that nothing but the utter annihilation of those iron men could give him possession of the place, called off his troops.

It was on such occasions as this, that the Old Guard showed its strength. Tried in a hundred battles, it had never betrayed the confidence of its great leader, and he knew when he sent them on that dreadful errand that they would fulfil it.

The Guard suffered heavily in these two conflicts, and while the army was shut up in the island of Lobau, the emperor took great care of it. When he broke up his quarters at Schoenbrun and removed to the island, his first visit was to them in their bivouacs where he found them at their repast. "Well, my friends," said he to a group before which he had stopped, "how do you find the wine?"

"It will not make us tipsy," replied an old grenadier, and pointing to the Danube, added, "behold our wine cellar."

Napoleon, who had ordered the distribution of a bottle of wine to each soldier of the Guard, was surprised to find that his commands had not been obeyed, and sending for Berthier, made him inquire into it. It being ascertained that those employed to furnish the wine had sold it for their own profit, they were immediately arrested, tried by a military commission, condemned, and executed. The punishment was sudden and severe upon any one who dared to trifle with his Old Guard. They might as well defraud or injure him.

The Guard at Wagram

At the opening of this great battle on the second day, the Old Guard, with the reserve cavalry, were stationed in the rear of the centre. Flushed by the successes of the day before, the Archduke had resumed the offensive, and descending the plateau, poured an enormous force on Napoleon's right. The latter stood and listened awhile to the heavy cannonading, but as the rapidly advancing roar of the enemy's artillery revealed that his right wing was forced back, he put spurs to his horse, and swiftly crossing the field with the Old Guard, was soon at the menaced point. The artillery, under the immortal Drouot, opened like a volcano on the advancing columns, smiting them in flank so terribly that they were forced to retreat. The cuirassiers then charged, carrying disorder and destruction into their ranks.

But while this was passing, a more imminent peril had overtaken the centre and left. Against both the Austrians were successful. The lion-hearted Massena, who commanded the left, was overturned in his carriage by his own panic-stricken troops. Unable to mount on horseback, filled with rage at the discomfiture of his men, he ordered the dragoons about his person to charge his flying soldiers as if they were enemies. But even this did not avail, and had not Napoleon's eagle eye discovered the condition of his favorite general, he would soon have been a prisoner in the hands of the enemy. Then passed one of those scenes that make us for awhile forget the carnage of a great battle field. From the extreme right, at first like a slowly ascending thunder-cloud, and then like a bolt from heaven, came Napoleon and his guard to the rescue. Ordering Davoust to attack Neusiedel, and the foot soldiers of the Guard to traverse the entire field at the "pas de charge," he took with him the squadrons of the steel-clad cuirassiers and the artillery of the Guard, and striking into a fierce gallop crossed the field in sight of both armies. That dread artillery, with Drouot in the midst, and those dark squadrons fringed with glittering steel, thundered after their great leader. The earth groaned and trembled as they passed, and even the combatants paused a moment as that apparition swept with a deep dull roar along. The French army gave a shout as they watched its headlong course. Soon after came the bear-skin caps of the foot grenadiers going almost on a run, though perfect in their formation as on parade.

Order was restored, and the shattered columns under the impenetrable wall which the Old Guard presented, rallied and executed the commands of Napoleon with the most perfect regularity, though riddled by the cross fire of the Austrian artillery. It was on this occasion that Napoleon on his white Persian charger rode backwards and forwards before his shrinking lines, to keep them steady while his other manœuvres could be executed. For a whole hour he and his indomitable Guard stood the rock of that battle-field. And when the crisis had come and Macdonald was directed to make that last awful charge on the Austrian centre, he took with him eight battalions of the Young Guard, while on either flank hovered the light horse, and at the head of his dread column advanced a hundred pieces of cannon of the Old Guard commanded by Drouot. Behind him, as a reserve, was the emperor surrounded by the cavalry and infantry of the Old Guard. Thus, with the Young Guard around him, and Napoleon and the Old Guard behind him, Drouot and his deadly artillery in front, Macdonald entered with a bold step the volcano before him. The particulars of that charge I have given in another place. Napoleon's throne and crown went with it. To sustain it Bessieres charged with the cavalry of the Old Guard and was hurled from his horse by a cannon shot which checked the enthusiasm of his troops and rendered the onset weak and powerless. But the day was won, thanks to the unconquerable Guard. In his bulletin Napoleon said:

> The artillery of the Guard has covered itself with glory. Our intrepid cannoneers have shown all the power of their terrible arm. The mounted chasseurs of the Guard have charged three squares of infantry and broken them in pieces. The Polish Lancers charged a regiment of Austrian lancers and took prisoner its commander, Prince D'Auesperg, and captured twelve pieces of cannon.

WAGRAM

The truth is, it is difficult to give a proper idea of the conduct of the Old Guard. To the cursory reader it seems strange that it acquired such a reputation. This arises from the fact that it always acted as a reserve, and had nothing to do with the main movements of the army, which it is the duty of the historian to describe. To stem the torrent of defeat, to give impulse to a great movement, to strengthen an exhausted column, and by being here and there and in every place where help was needed, and with unbroken front in the midst of disorder and calm resolute hearts in the midst of fear and panic, that it gained its renown.

The discomfited soldier gazed in astonishment on the cool courage which triumphed where he had failed, and broken ranks viewed with wonder the steady march on batteries which had shattered them to fragments. Called in only when the other troops gave way, and manœuvring and charging with the same determined bravery in the midst of a panic as in the flush of victory, they were looked upon as superior to the ordinary emotions and fears of mortals. And nothing does show the sublime elevation of this invincible body of men more than their freedom from the contagion of example, being always sufficient in themselves, and steadiest and bravest the moment of greatest disaster and fear.

It was this peculiarity that gave the Guard influence over the soldiers and made its presence like the shout of victory. The whole army came to regard it as exempt from ordinary duty in a battle-field, too great to be employed in ordinary fighting, and to be called upon only when the bravest troops gave way. Its charge was looked upon as an unalterable decree against the enemy written in the book of fate. Its stern and measured tread never faltered, against its adamantine sides cavalry thundered in vain, while before its levelled bayonets the firmest array went down. Napo-

leon knew its power and increased its strength to the greatest limit it could bear. Any nation that could furnish two
hundred thousand men able to fulfil the severe conditions
annexed to admission in the Old Guard, might conquer
the world.

The battle of Wagram settled the fate of Austria, and not
long after the "peace of Vienna" was concluded. The war in
the Tyrol and Spain was carried on, but the majority of the
Old Guard took no part in either. They were sent back to
Paris to recruit.

In 1809, the Guard was composed of 31,203 men.

CHAPTER 6

1810

In 1810 the star of Bonaparte culminated. It was perhaps the most glorious year of his life. He had compelled peace from the continental powers, and the French empire had been extended on one side to the mouth of the Elbe, and on the other to the shores of the Tiber. Rome and Amsterdam were both cities of the Empire. Joseph Bonaparte was king of Spain, Jerome of Westphalia, and Murat of Naples. Napoleon was king of Italy as well as Emperor of France, and was looked up to with awe by a hundred million men. Kings gazed with amazement and fear on this strange man, who made such playthings of their thrones, and dictated terms to them in their own palaces, and whose victorious armies trod the streets of their capitals. This plebeian soldier had changed the contempt with which royal blood regarded him, into deadly fear; and he whom they deemed fit only for the assassin's knife, was now worthy of the haughtiest alliance, and the daughter of the Caesars became the wife of Napoleon.

It is strange how slight an event will change the features of the world. Napoleon first proposed to marry one of the royal family of Russia. The emperor was delighted with the project, but the queen-mother suggested difficulties, and demanded delay. This did not suit the impetuous nature of Bonaparte, and he immediately broke off negotiations with Russia and offered himself to the house of Austria, and was accepted. This latter alliance, from which he hoped so much, proved of no benefit to him, except to facilitate his operations against Russia, which in the end proved his ruin. Austria regards family ties no more than treaties or honor. Treacherous and base, no reliance can be placed on her fidelity to any thing but her self interest.

Russia on the other hand, had the two dynasties been united, would have proved a close ally to France. That fearful invasion of her territories would have been prevented, and the two emperors could have divided Europe between them, if they chose, and prostrated England in the dust.

The last war with Austria had impressed Napoleon still more deeply with the value of the Old Guard, and he took advantage of the first interval of peace to augment its strength. Holland had fallen into his hands, and he incorporated into his Guard the grenadiers of the Holland Guard. He created also musical corps for the eight regiments of the Young Guard already in existence, and doubled the officers of health attached to the chief hospital. In two years he had more than doubled its number.

Review of the Imperial Guard

Napoleon frequently entertained the Parisians with a grand review of his troops, especially of his Guard. This always took place on the Sabbath, to give all an opportunity of witnessing it, just as that day has ever been made a sort of fete day by the French. On the 3d of June, of this year, he held one of these grand reviews in presence of the dignitaries of the empire, and ambassadors from almost every court of Europe. A chamberlain of the emperor of Russia, the count of Trawinsoff, was then at the French court, ostensibly to enroll a troupe of comedians for the imperial theatre of St. Petersburg. He was accredited simply as a charge, but Napoleon knew perfectly well that graver matters than a troope of comedians were entrusted to him. On the morning of the review of his Guard, he asked him to be present and give his opinion of it. The count having no desire to see the redoubtable corps which at Austerlitz and Eylau had conquered the finest troops of his master, declined on the ground that he had no horse. The emperor replied he would give him one of his own, and the count was compelled to accept the invitation. As the clock struck twelve, there arose from the different corps of the Guard which some time before had taken position in the court of the Tuileries, a loud murmur of expectation succeeded by a profound silence. The rattling of a scabbard and the clicking of spurs as the booted heel came down upon the marble floor of the peristyle was heard, and the next moment a little man in a green uniform, the modest epaulettes of a colonel on his shoulders, a plain chapeau on his head, the signs of the Legion of Honor, and the crown of iron, the only ornaments on his breast, stepped forth. He paused and made a gesture with his hand, and in a few seconds a group of officers in splendid uniforms, with their hats in their hands, surrounded him. The drums then beat the salute, a single command like an echo rolled from officer to officer the whole length of the line, and with a clattering sound, the entire army as if it had been one man, presented arms—the colors in one vast cloud stooped towards that little man in green uniform, and "Vive l' Empereur," rolled like thunder to the heavens.

Napoleon then mounted his favorite horse Marengo, whose head was always in motion as if impatient like his master to be off on a gallop, and rode along the lines. Just as he was about to pass into the ranks, a young man seventeen or eighteen years of age, rushed out of the multitude and ran towards him, shaking a paper which he held in his hand above his head. Paying no heed to the repeated order of "back, back," he was pushing on, when a grenadier seized him by the collar and forced him towards the spectators. But he still shook his paper and cried out over the noise of the multitude, "Sire, Sire," to the emperor.

The latter said coldly, "Let the young man approach."

The grenadier immediately released him, and presenting arms stood like a statue. The young man sprang forward and fell at the feet of Marengo.

"What do you want?" said Napoleon, as he stooped in his saddle to take the paper. The poor petitioner said nothing, but looked beseechingly at the emperor, while the tears rolled down his cheeks. Napoleon tore off the envelope and casting his eye over the petition, said to the young man, "Arise, to none but God should you kneel; from what I see, your mother has never left Paris." There was no reply and casting his eye again on the paper, he said in a low voice, "I have been deceived respecting this woman who I was told had emigrated and then mixed herself up in political intrigues. There was nothing in it." Then raising his voice, he added, "My young friend, tell your mother that from this moment she has a pension of twelve hundred francs from my own purse."

Overwhelmed by this sudden elevation from the depths of despair, the poor youth stood a moment, while the hue of death crept over his features, his eyes closed and sinking on his knees he pitched forward, his head striking heavily against the legs of Marengo as he fell. The frightened steed reared bolt upright and but for an aid-de- camp, who seized him by the bridle, would doubtless have flung his imperial rider. A cry of terror rose from the multitude, but the next moment as they saw him quietly dismount and advance towards the young man, there went up a shout that shook the field.

An officer immediately called aloud for a surgeon. "Let him alone, sir," said Napoleon quietly, "a surgeon is useless, joy is never fatal at this age. He needs only a little cool water." One of the spectators ran and fetched some in his hat from a neighboring fountain. Napoleon threw a few drops on the poor fellow's face when he opened his eyes. Seeing the emperor stooping over him, he seized one of his hands and kissed it in a transport of enthusiasm. "Was not I right?" said Napoleon pleasantly. "To horse, gentlemen." At evening that youth sent another petition, that he might fight till death for the emperor. He was enrolled in the foot chasseurs of the Guard.

This to an ordinary general would be an unimportant affair, yet many a victory of Napoleon grew out of just such incidents. This young chasseur would be worth a whole company in a desperate charge. With the eye of his benefactor on him, nothing but death could arrest his progress, and his example in battle would make heroes of all around him.

At the time this was transpiring, another incident of a comic character, yet equally illustrative of Napoleon's love for the brave, and of his tact in winning their unbounded devotion, occurred in another part of the field. Gros, one of the generals of the chasseurs of the Old Guard, was a tall, powerful man, with a voice like a trumpet. He was illiterate, but high-minded, generous to a fault, and the very soul of bravery. Napoleon once said of him, "Gros lives in the smoke of cannon like a fish in water. It is his element." The mode of his elevation to the rank he held, was a farce in itself. One morning while he was waiting in one of the little saloons of St. Cloud to receive the orders of the Emperor, who had sent for him, he became impatient at the long delay and ,going up to a mirror, began to contemplate himself. He pulled up his collar, adjusted his epaulettes, examined his uniform, and casting his eyes from his head to his feet, could not repress his admiration of the tout ensemble of his person and thinking aloud, said, "Ah my cadet, there are few of these dandy officers made up like you—what a misfortune you don't know a little mathematics which the emperor requires, you would then have been a general to-day." Napoleon who had entered unperceived and overheard this queer soliloquy, suddenly slapped him on the shoulder exclaiming, "You are one."

On the day of the review, Gros with his regiment was at one extremity of the line. A few days before there had been incorporated into it unbeknown to him an old friend named Castagnet. He was a drummer and in the review was placed in the front rank. Gros with great pomposity was slowly walking his horse along the line, scrutinizing the appearance and arms of each, when he was suddenly arrested by "Good heavens! it is you, my general, look at me, I am that fool of a Castagnet with whom you have drunk more Schnick than there is broth in the kettle of the Invalids. How are you? Don't you know me, my general?"

At the first words, Gros had recognised his old comrade, and yielding to the sudden generous impulse, he leaped from his horse and embraced him, shaking his hand with a grasp that made every bone in it snap, exclaiming, "Very well, very well, my old Castagnet, and you?"

"Always *r-r-r-rat-a-tat tatting*, as you see."

"Come to me to-morrow morning," said Gros as he remounted his horse, "you shall see that I always have something for my old friends."

Napoleon, who had just gone through the first files of the grenadiers, happened to cast his eye along the line at this moment and thought he saw a soldier and general embracing each other. The spurs sank in the flanks of Marengo, which sprang away like a flash of lightning, and the next moment stood before the astonished group.

The Imperial Guard

"What does this mean, General Gros," exclaimed Napoleon, with his brow knit in anger, "is this a theatrical exhibition?"

The general raised his chapeau, and pointing to the drummer, who stood immovable in his ranks, said in his usual frank blunt manner, "There is a solid soldier for you, one who never winks in presence of the enemy. Such as you see him, sire, he has beat his drum in Italy, Egypt, and through all Germany. Hi name is Castagnet. It was he who beat the charge before St. Jean d'Acre with one hand because the other had been shattered by a ball, at the commencement of that earthquake."

As much as Napoleon loved discipline, he loved bravery better, and he sat with his eyes fixed on Castagnet, whose heart went like the sticks of his own drum, while Gros was speaking; and as he finished said, "All this is very well, but the time is ill chosen for such recognitions." Then turning to Castagnet, he said in that winning tone which so bewitched his soldiers, "You are he then, my brave fellow, who descended the third time into the fosse of St. Jean d'Acre; I am glad to see you again." With this he lifted his hand to his chapeau, slightly raising it from his head.

These flattering words, and above all, the gesture of respect, completely upset the poor drummer. He expected punishment, and lo, the emperor had touched his chapeau to him. He turned white and red by turns, and turning and twisting his head about, said, in a half audible tone, "You flatter me, my emperor."

"It was you," continued Napoleon, "I have a good memory, who showed such presence of mind and admirable courage at the battle of Wertingnen, and saved the life of your captain."

The brave fellow whose nerves were steady as iron in the deadly combat, was completely unmanned, and with his head cast down, said in a voice lower than before, "A small affair, my emperor, always the same old cask."

"Gros," added Napoleon, "if your protege continues to behave as well in future, he shall be advanced. He is worthy of a better post," and nodding pleasantly to the drummer, said, "Au revoir, my brave fellow," and gave the spur to Marengo.

Such was the means by which Napoleon gained the hearts of his Guard. The beat of that brave fellow's drum in the fosse of St. Jean d'Acre would not hurry men to the deadly charge more fiercely than that story told by the bivouac fire of the Old Guard at night. The whole regiment witnessed the strange scene, and there was not a man in it but felt a higher resolution. He would carry the remembrance of it into battle, it would nerve him to another effort when about to give way, and rally him to another charge at sight of his commander. Who would not perform great deeds, when years after he was told of them by his emperor, in presence of the whole army? The brave acts of even a poor drummer were treasured up in the heart of him for whom he shed his blood, and it recompensed him for all he had suffered. Ah, Bonaparte knew how to win the hearts of his soldiers, and that alone would give him unconquerable troops.

After having passed in review the squadrons of the Guard and the light cavalry, he returned to the court of the Tuileries, and placed himself in front of a small squadron of general officers, composed of his staff. At a gesture of his hand, an officer of ordnance approached with his head uncovered, and bowing to Napoleon, parted on a gallop and riding rapidly along the whole front of battle returned to his place. A moment after Napoleon urged Marengo, covered with foam, a few steps in advance, and lifting his hand shook it above his head. From the extreme end of the line the faint roll of drums was heard, gradually swelling, till it swept like thunder over the field. In an instant it ceased and the rattling of musketry ran with the regularity of a wave, from one end of the vast line to the other. At length the impassible face of Napoleon kindled with excitement; and placing his right hand upon his thigh, he half turned in his saddle, and gave the Russian ambassador, who was absorbed in the magnificent tableau, a glance that could not be mistaken. He had caught the undulations of the eagles of his Guard as it put itself in motion, and from the farthest extremity, began to advance. The foot grenadiers and chasseurs, who had swept the fields of Austerlitz, Jena, Eylau, and Wagram, first approached. As they began to defile, Napoleon made a sign to the Russian chamberlain to take his place by his side. As the regiments approached, he said, pointing to one, "That is my 45th, they are my brave children of Paris. If ever cartridges are burned between my brother, the emperor of Russia, and me, I will show the efficiency of my 45th. It was this regiment that precipitated itself upon the Russian batteries at Austerlitz. That little corporal you see running there with his fusil upon his shoulder, finding himself about to be taken by an officer of the cannoneers of Doctorow, sprang up behind him, strangled him with his hands, and made his escape." The chamberlain expressing his admiration of the daring deed, Napoleon added, "There is not a regiment in my Guard that cannot cite a hundred acts far more admirable. Do you see that lieutenant covered with dust? It is Robaglia, my cousin, who lives but for me." He thus went on particularizing one after another, going back even to his first campaigns.

The cavalry then defiled in the same wonderful order, though enveloped in a cloud of dust. The terrible grenadiers, whose heavy shocks few squares could withstand, passed along, followed by the chasseurs with their green uniform and tall plumes waving like a field of grain in the wind. After them, the Mamelukes, with their white turbans surmounted with a cross of gold, then the dragoons of the Guard, with their light helmets flashing in the sun, commanded by Arigha, a cousin of Napoleon, then the Polish lancers in their gay and sparkling uniform, and last the artillery of the Guard, followed by the equipages of the train. Each regiment and squadron sent up their loud "Vive l' Empereur," as it passed. Napoleon then dismounted and mixing with the chief officers of the several corps, conversed a while familiarly with them and returned to the Tuileries.

The imposing pageant had passed. That army of thirty thousand warriors—veterans every one, had moved at the word of command, like a single man, and no one who saw their firm array and perfect discipline, and knew their history, could be astonished at their invincibility. When it was over, Napoleon asked the Russian chamberlain what had struck him most at the review.

"The prodigious memory of your majesty," he replied, "and the ease with which you recalled, after so long a time, the deeds of arms and the names of so many soldiers."

"Monsieur Count," replied the emperor, "it is the memory of the heart, it is that of the lover which recalls his first attachments, it is never lost."

I have thus gone into a detailed account of this single review, because such exhibitions formed a part of the history of the Old Guard, and incidents like these I have related lay at the foundation of the devoted attachment it showed to Napoleon.

At the close of 1810 the Guard numbered 33,500 men.

CHAPTER 7

1811

In March, 1811, the regiment of the Young Holland-
ers, formed by Louis Bonaparte, King of Holland, at the
abdication of the latter, were called, as before stated, into
France, and incorporated into the Young Guard. At first it
was composed of only two battalions but afterwards was increased to nine, and gave an addition to the Guard of nine
thousand men.

The birth of a son to Napoleon, filled the nation with
joy, and removed from the statesman of France a load of
anxiety. The French empire and Napoleon were one. He
had made it, and he alone could preserve its integrity. No
other statesman nor leader in the army, even if elevated
to his place, could sway his sceptre. Were he dead, France
must look into the gulf of another revolution, or submit
to the dictation of tyrants. And yet this single man, on
whose shoulders lay the interests of so vast an empire,
lived on the battle-field, exposed to death on every side.
Wise men trembled when they saw so mighty a struc-
ture resting on a single pedestal, and asked, what would
become of France if the shot that pierced the breast of
Turenne, or shattered Charles XII., should pierce him. A
son would confirm his dynasty, and the army would rally
around his cradle, for the father's sake. It was from such

views sprung the strong desire on the part of France, that Napoleon should be divorced from Josephine and marry some one who could give him an heir. One can, therefore, easily imagine the intoxication of the French people when that heir was actually born.

The confinement of the queen was known throughout Paris, and the whole population was on the tip-toe of expectation. At length the cannon of the Invalides thundered forth the joyful event that a child was born. It was announced beforehand that if it were a princess, twenty-one guns should be fired—if a prince, a hundred. As the first heavy explosion rolled over the city, the vast population stood and listened. They counted to the twenty-first discharge, at which there was a pause. The excitement then became intense and when at length the twenty-second gun, double charged, pealed over the Seine, a wild shout of enthusiasm shook the capital to its centre, telling to all Europe how deep-seated was the affection of the people for their Emperor, and how great their joy at the prospect of the continuation of his dynasty.

The birth of this young "king of Rome," as he was titled, was celebrated with extraordinary pomp.

To give greater eclat to the event, and at the same time form the nucleus of a Guard which should be to his son what the Old Guard had been to him, he issued a decree, creating a regiment of two battalions composed of six companies each, under the name of pupils of the Guard, to be called "Guards of the King of Rome." The young Bonaparte was to be the commander when he became old enough to handle a sword. No one could be admitted into this guard under ten, or over sixteen years of age. He also must be the son or nephew of a soldier who had died on the field of battle. He must be able to read and write, and bring proof that he had been vaccinated. Most of the officers were chosen from the military school of St. Cyr—and from the sub-lieutenants, up to the colonel commandant, they were nominated by the emperor himself; after being proposed by the minister of war. This corps of boys was organized at Versailles, and very soon numbered four thousand. They were all orphans, and Napoleon said, "their fathers being dead, the army shall be their father." They had a standard of their own, but no eagle; for that was never given to a regiment unless earned on the field of battle.

After they had been drilled awhile, the emperor ordered them to be brought to Paris from Versailles, to figure in one of his grand reviews of the Old Guard. The latter were drawn up in line of battle, when to the surprise of every one, a new army in miniature debouched by the bridge royal, and advanced in good order in front of the troops. The martial air and erect figures of these boys of ten to sixteen years of age astonished every one. There was a platoon of sappers, little fair-haired urchins, with bear-skin caps whose beardless chins and lively faces contrasted ludicrously with the terrible air they tried to give themselves. The drum-major was five feet two inches high, and as he passed the Old Guard, he made his cane fly about his head with extraordinary rapidity, as much as to say, "beat that if you can. He was followed by the drummers, but without the larger bass drums, for there were none big enough to beat them. They played "la Favorite," a quick step composed expressly for them. Then came the chief officers on horseback, followed by the whole corps. As they marched along, they looked for all the world like the Old Guard seen through an inverted spy glass. They formed in front of the 1st regiment of grenadiers, and the old veterans at the sight of these baby soldiers laughed and chuckled in great delight.

Soon, however, the beat of drums announced the arrival of the Emperor, who appeared on the field and rode straight to the pupils. They opened their ranks to receive him, and he dismounted, and, accompanied by the little staff officers, began his inspection. All at once he stopped, and seizing a corporal by the ear, pulled him towards him, and, in a stern voice, asked his age.

"Thirteen years old, my Emperor, the 30th of last March, the day of the birth of the King of Rome."

"Why did you smile just now when I spoke to your captain?"

"From pleasure in seeing you," replied the little blond.

"And what, if on arriving at Versailles, I should have you put in the hall of police, to teach you that an under officer never ought to smile in the ranks?"

"My Emperor, it would make me very happy, for it would show that you had thought of me."

Napoleon smiled at the naive reply, and passed on.

After he had finished his inspection, he ordered the line of pupils to advance a few steps, then placing himself between them and his grenadiers, he said:

"Soldiers of my Old Guard, behold your children! Their fathers fell fighting by your sides, and you will take their places to them. They will find in you, at the same time, an example and a support. Be their tutors. In imitating you, they will be brave; in listening to your counsel, they will become the first soldiers of the world. I confide to them the Guard of my son. With them I will have no fear for him, as with you I am without fear for myself. I ask for them your friendship and protection."

"Vive l'Empereur! Vive le Roi de Rome!" rolled in deafening shouts through the ranks.

Napoleon, with a gesture of his hand, checked their enthusiasm, and, turning to the pupils, said, in a subdued tone,

"And you, my children, in attaching you to my Guard, I have given you a difficult duty to fulfill; but I rely upon you, and I hope one day to hear it said — 'These children are worthy of their fathers.'"

As he finished, the most frantic acclamations rent the air.

He little thought, that in less than three years he would see those children crushing Russian grenadiers beneath their impetuous charge, and leaving their youthful forms on the soil of France in bravely endeavoring to hurl back the invaders of her soil.

As the troops defiled before him, the pupils were at the head of the Old Guard, and throughout the parade marched in good order, like trained soldiers. As the grenadiers came opposite Napoleon, a child of ten years old quitted his comrades, and advancing timidly towards him, presented, at a distance, his little bonnet, on which was placed a petition.

"Ah, ha!" said Napoleon, smiling, "ambitious already. He has commenced early." Then turning to Lauriston, his aide, he bade him see what the child wanted. As the latter brought back the petition, he said: "Sire, it is an orphan."

"An orphan!" interrupted the Emperor; "then I must see to it. Give me the paper."

As he unrolled the petition, he saw it was addressed to his infant child. It began:

To his Majesty the King of Rome
Sire: Pierre Muscadet, eleven campaigns old, exclusive proprietor of five wounds not mortal, and foot grenadier of the Old Guard to your honored father, who has decorated the petitioner with his own hands at Boulogne, wishes to let you know that he has a nephew with whom he knows not what to do, inasmuch as he wishes to become a soldier. He is of blond complexion; has been vaccinated according to the rules. The bearer will undoubtedly make a good soldier.

He knows how to read and write, and is aware of the respect due to his chiefs, and to the heir presumptive to the great Napoleon. The petitioner, therefore, prays that you will have the goodness to permit his nephew, Francois Muscadet, bearer of the present, to be incorporated as soon as possible into the corps of the pupils of the Guard, which is your own. I promise that he will never murmur in the service of your imperial person, royal and Roman.

The old soldier made his sign at the bottom of the petition.

In reading it, Napoleon smiled again and again. As he read the address, "To his Majesty the King of Rome," he shrugged his shoulders and said, "But this is not for me."

Having made a sign for the boy to approach, he said, "Thou art called Francis, and art nephew of Pierre Muscadet, grenadier of my Guard?"

"Yes, my Emperor," he replied, timidly, rolling his bonnet in his hands.

"Well, tell your uncle that he is a simpleton."

"Yes, my Emperor," replied the little fellow, with his eyes cast down.

Napoleon smiled at his naivete, and continued, "Nevertheless, his commission shall be punctually executed, for it would not be right to let you be the victim of your uncle's foolishness." Then turning to his aide-de-camp, he said, "Take the petitioner with his petition to my son."

Lauriston introduced the little Francis into the chamber of his Majesty, then five months old. He was asleep, but just then waking up, began to cry vociferously. Lauriston thinking his commission fulfilled, returned and found Napoleon occupied with the movements of the light artillery.

"Well," said he, "have you done what I desired?"

"Yes, sire."

"What response did his Majesty the King of Rome make?"

"Sire, his Majesty made no reply." Napoleon smiled and said, "They say silence gives consent. I will see to it this evening." Then turning to Francis, he bade him rejoin his comrades, and take care not to get under the horses' feet. He watched him as he ran with all his might through the ranks of the last battalion of grenadiers, and when he lost sight of him he said, "Poor little fellow, I wager that he will be no fool; but his uncle, though simple, is not less one of my braves, and I wish to gratify him."

Afterwards when Napoleon was disputing inch by inch the soil of France against an overwhelming army, this Francis led his troops to the charge with the sang-froid of a veteran, and equalled the Old Guard in a murderous action on the plains of Champagne. Although wounded early in the battle, he refused to quit the field, but lay bleeding and shouting, "Vive l' Empereur," till the Russians gave way. The cross of the Legion of Honor was his reward.

Immediately after the review, the pupils of the Guard commenced their service around the young king of Rome. The ladies in waiting of the empress amused themselves much with these miniature soldiers, teasing and consoling them by turns. Like the Old Guard, in its service to the Emperor, a portion only was on duty at a time, relieving the other every day. In the morning when the new detachment arrived, it found in its cartouch boxes, tops, toys, balls filled with bon bons and confectionery of every description. Such playthings did they make of these unfledged soldiers whom Ney himself two years after was to lead with astonishment against the veterans of Europe.

At the close of this year, 1811, the Guard numbered 51,960 men.

CHAPTER 8

1812: the Guard in Russia

The world never saw such a spectacle, and probably never will behold one like it in the future, as Europe presented in the spring of 1812. The vast intellect of Napoleon had not only triumphed over the surrounding sovereigns so long banded against him, but had compelled them to assist him in the accomplishment of his great plans, and Italy, Austria, Russia, Bavaria, Poland, Holland, and Sweden, sent up his war-cry. The flags that had so long advanced against each other in deadly combat, waved side by side in friendly greeting. Regiments that had last seen each other as they met in mortal strife and fierce hate at Marengo, Austerlitz, Jena, and Wagram, now swore to move shoulder to shoulder in a common cause. The lion of the north was to be bearded in his den, and Napoleon with 500,000 men at his back, started for Moscow. The magnitude and grandeur of the expedition filled the world with amazement, and thousands of the wealthy and noble eagerly sought a place in it to partake of the glory that awaited it. From the Baltic to the Calabrian mountains, and from the Atlantic to the Vistula, the nations obeyed one imperious will and thronged at his command to one banner. The gathering of troops from every quarter to a common centre, the highways of

France and Germany crowded for months with infantry, cavalry, and artillery, pouring in endless thousands forward, imparted to every beholder the feeling of invincible power. A half a million of men, eighty thousand cavalry, thirteen hundred cannon thundering heavily along, a hundred and eighty-seven thousand horses, twenty thousand chariots and wagons, these formed the spectacle on which the gaze of nations was riveted. More than all, at the head of this vast and imposing array, rode the greatest chieftain of ancient or modern times, one who occupied an elevation no monarch since Caesar had reached, and under whose control in various parts of the continent marched 1,400,000 men. But accustomed as he was to vast undertakings, the magnitude of this had filled him with serious misgivings. Besides, he was acting directly contrary to the rule which he himself had laid down, viz., to do one thing at a time, and strike in a mass. But here he had Spain in his hands where many of his best troops were engaged, and at the same time was marching against the extreme north, thus keeping two fires blazing at opposite extremities, which always threaten to exhaust and consume the centre.

Napoleon, however, had a grand army under his control. He had augmented his Guard to upwards of fifty-six thousand men, a large army in itself. The Consular Guard at Marengo, of eight hundred men, presents a striking contrast to this immense host. But the "column of granite" had not changed its character, and as it first stood on the disordered battle-field so firm and immovable, it still stood,—the rock which the sea lashes in vain.

In the advance to Moscow, Napoleon spared his Guard. Battle after battle was fought, and these brave troops were compelled to look on as idle spectators. It was no better in the "battle of giants."

At Borodino the Guard had pitched their tents about the Emperor, expecting in the morning they at least might do something worthy of their old renown. But in the most critical state of the battle that followed, he held them back. At noon, Murat and Ney had opened the road to victory, but were too exhausted to occupy it without reinforcements, and sent to the Emperor for them. But the fever which wasted him had quenched the life and fiery vigor he always exhibited on the field of battle, and he remained listless, as if under a spell a great part of the time. He could not make up his mind to grant Ney and Murat's request. He pondered long with himself, and after again and again giving the order for the Young Guard to advance, he each time countermanded it and kept it near his person.

Those two fiery leaders who had struggled so gloriously, and saw victory in their grasp, were compelled by this strange delay to halt, while the enemy reformed, and attacked them in turn. After driving every thing before them, they found themselves scarce able to make good their defence against the heavy onsets to which they were exposed. Again Murat sent an urgent demand for succor, and Napoleon at length promised the Young Guard. But it had scarcely begun to advance when he ordered it to halt. Count Lobau, however, under the pretence of dressing the line, worked it gradually forward, which the Emperor observing, repeated his order. He did, however, let the artillery of the Guard advance, which soon told with frightful effect on the enemy.

The generals had been amazed at the unwonted apathy of their great leader, and it was with joy, therefore, they saw eighty pieces of this renowned artillery lining the summits, and opening their heavy fire like a single gun. The Russian cavalry, shattered by it, were compelled to retire behind the infantry. The latter then advanced in black and heavy mass-

BORODINO

es. Through these the cannon balls made wide and fearful rents. But they were closed up as fast as made, and stern and steady the iron columns continued to advance until they came within reach of grape shot, when the batteries smote them like a sudden hail-storm. Whole companies fell at every discharge. Every where throughout the ranks portions were seen suddenly to sink away as if engulfed in the earth.

The soldiers, however, nobly endeavored to maintain their formation, closing steadily over the dead bodies, and trampling them under foot. But they could not breast that frightful tempest, driving its iron sleet in their very faces; and they halted, and either petrified at the awful destruction around them, or from want of presence of mind and generalship on the part of their leaders, they stood for two hours crushed by this deadly fire, making no effort to advance or retreat. Not a single movement was visible throughout the immense mass during the whole time, except what was made by the falling ranks.

The brave artillerymen of the Guard at length got tired of this horrible slaughter, and the French infantry advanced and swept the field. Ney, Murat, and Davoust, commanding the right wings now pushed steadily forward, and annihilated half of the Russian line, and came upon the uncovered flank of the remainder. Feeling themselves not strong enough to meet the whole army, they called aloud for the Young Guard. "The Young Guard!" they exclaimed, "only let it follow them at a distance. Let it show itself, and take its place upon the heights. They themselves would then finish it." General Belliard was again sent to Napoleon for it, but the latter still hesitated.

When Belliard returned to Murat and reported the indecision of the Emperor, saying that he "found him still seated in the same place, with a suffering and dejected air, his features sunken, and gazing around him with a dull look, and giving his orders languishingly in the midst of these dreadful warlike noises, to which he seemed completely a stranger," he was sad. He, however, understood it, for he had seen him the day before halt several times and dismount, and lean his head upon a cannon, apparently in deep suffering. Sickness had prostrated him. But Ney, who was ignorant of this, was thrown into a rage, and exclaimed, "Are we come so far, then, to be satisfied only with a field of battle? What business has the Emperor in the rear of the army? There he is only within reach of reverses, and not of victory."

Not long after, Napoleon was told that the cry from the whole army was for the Guard, to which he replied, "And if there should be another battle tomorrow, where will be my army to fight it?"

Again, for the fourth time, Murat sent to him, asking only for the cavalry of the Guard. With them he would turn the entranced heights, with their terrible redoubt, which offered almost insuperable obstacles in front, and against which Eugene was endeavoring to advance under a most destructive fire from the artillery. He still delayed till it was too late to take advantage of the crisis into which affairs had been thrown. That redoubt, however, which had engulfed so many brave French soldiers, must be carried, or the battle be lost; and Murat ordered Caulincourt, who succeeded Montbrun in the command of the first division of cavalry, after the latter fell, to charge the Russian line, and breaking through it, dash into the great redoubt by the gorge in rear, and storm the battery that was mowing down the ranks of Eugene.

This brave officer was general in the Guard, and the whole night before the battle had lain awake on the floor, wrapped in his cloak, gazing on the miniature of his young wife, whom he had married but a week previous to his departure from Paris. He was sad and depressed, and seemed to have a foreboding of the fate that awaited him. As he put himself at the head of the cavalry, he found the aides-de-camp of Montbrun in tears at the loss of their commander. "Follow me," said he: "weep not for him, but come and avenge his death." In reply to Murat's order to enter that redoubt right through the Russian line, he said, "You shall soon see me there, dead or alive."

The bugles sounded the charge, and putting himself at the head of this splendid corps of cavalry, he dashed forward in a gallop. The Russians saw the coming tempest, and advanced several regiments around the menaced point to meet it, while the plunging fire from the redoubt smote the swiftly-advancing column in flank. Heedless of all, young Caulincourt pressed forward with loud cheers, and fiercely riding down the Russian cavalry sent to meet him, stormed over the solid masses of infantry, then suddenly wheeling to the left with the heavy-armed cuirassiers, while the light cavalry was left to occupy the discomfited infantry, began to ascend the slopes towards that terrible redoubt.

Eugene had just been driven out of it with dreadful slaughter, and with reformed columns was again advancing to the attack. His bayonets were already gleaming along the ascent, when the driving column of the cuirassiers, enveloped in smoke, was seen fiercely scaling the highest summit. The sides of that hill were for a moment "clothed in glittering steel," the next under a redoubled fire from all the batteries, those fearless riders plunged straight into the volcano. Eugene, who had caught a glimpse of the column as it glittered along the sides of the hill, was filled with dread when he saw it disappear in that gloomy redoubt which lay curtained in smoke. But in a few seconds its thunder suddenly ceased, for its "fires were quenched in blood," and as the smoke slowly rolled away, there flashed in the sun the shining helmets of the cuirassiers, while a shout long and loud arose from its top. But Caulincourt found there his grave—struck by a musket ball as he was leading his men into the entrance, he fell dead in the very moment of victory. He was buried in the redoubt he had so nobly won.

He was brother to the grand equerry of Napoleon. When the victory, together with its loss, was reported to the Emperor, he turned to Caulincourt and said, "You have heard the news, do you wish to retire?" Overwhelmed with grief, the grand equerry made no reply, but slightly raising his hat, as if to thank him, he moved forward, while the big tears rolled silently down his cheeks. Caulincourt's death was a great loss to the Guard, and bitterly did they lament him.

At the close of the battle, Ney and Murat sent again for the Guard to complete the victory, but it was not given them, and the enemy retired in good order, leaving Napoleon a barren triumph.

At night, Napoleon called Mortier to him, and ordered him to advance with the Young Guard, but on no account pass the ravine which divided the two armies—he was simply to guard the field of battle. He even called him back to make sure that he understood his orders. An hour after he sent again, commanding him neither to advance nor retreat, whatever might happen.

At ten o'clock, the impetuous Murat, whom twelve hours of hard fighting could not exhaust, went himself to Napoleon saying that the enemy were crossing the Moskwa in great disorder, and asked for the cavalry of the Guard to finish it. The latter checked the ardor of his brother-in-law, and sat down to dictate the bulletin. The Old Guard encamped in solemn silence around him, but being aroused by an irruption of Cossacks, they were compelled to stand to arms, thus showing how meagre the victory had been.

The Retreat from Moscow

In the morning Napoleon rode over the wreck-covered field. A cold fierce wind, a driving rain, and a sombre sky, imparted still greater gloom and desolation to the scene. The hills and valleys were literally ploughed up, and the dead lay everywhere. The wounded Russians were dragging themselves wearily to the piles of the dead for shelter from the storm, while low moans arose on every side. The bivouacs of the French were silent, and officers and soldiers were gathered in scattered groups around their eagles, sad and sombre as the scene. As Napoleon passed gloomily along, he was compelled to trample on heaps of dead men. His escort did the same— and the hoofs of one of the horses coming down on a soldier not quite dead, extorted a low cry of pain. On hearing it Napoleon gave a sudden shriek—the first sound that had escaped his lips since he had begun to traverse the field.

He has been much blamed for withholding his Guard in the several crises of this battle. Segur has drawn him as utterly indifferent to its progress, as sitting with drooping head and stolid countenance during the whole of it. This is doubtless exaggeration. He evidently was not himself on that day—a sick man never is. There are times when the body will triumph over the soul, I care not what its capacity. Still Napoleon had reasons for what he did. He was nearly 2,000 miles from Paris, in an inhospitable country— far removed from his supplies, and he dared not risk his last hope. If the Guard was severely crippled, the army would be completely hors de combat.

Besides, he expected that the decisive battle would take place on the plains of Moscow—that there by the cradle of the Empire the army would make its last great stand, and in such a contingency he wanted at least the Guard intact, to meet any new reinforcements Alexander might bring against him. On the other hand, if by bringing up his resources he could have annihilated the army, the anticipated battle could not have been fought, nor would the enemy have been able to harass his retreat as it did. There were two sides to the question, which Napoleon, no doubt, weighed well. At all events Bessieres, the commander of the Guard, used all his influence to induce the Emperor to spare it, and he would not have done this without good reasons, for he was not one to stand idle, and hear the murmurs of his officers and men demanding to be led where honor and glory could be won, without his judgment told him it was imperiously necessary.

The next day, Napoleon put Mortier with a part of the Young Guard under Murat, who went in pursuit of the enemy. They overtook him near Krymskoie, established in a strong position. Murat was for instantly attacking, but Mortier expostulated with him, showing plainly that it would be madness. But Murat, heedless of everything, plunged on, thus compelling Mortier to second his efforts, or see his superior officer sacrificed. The result was as Mortier had predicted—they were repulsed with heavy loss, and two thousand of that reserve which had been husbanded so carefully at Borodino, were uselessly sacrificed. The same sacrifice on the field of battle, would doubtless have annihilated the Russian army.

But Moscow, the goal for which Napoleon had toiled over so many battlefields, was at last won, and he sat down in the Kremlin—the Old Guard occupying another portion of the same magnificent edifice.

The conflagration of the city followed. But after the fire had spread on every side, and finally attacked the Kremlin itself, and when a spark dropping on a single powder wagon would have hurled him and the Guard he had reared so carefully, into eternity, and after he was told that the Kremlin was undermined and ready to lift at the first touch of fire and bury all beneath the ruins, he obstinately clung to it for twenty-four hours. The Old Guard were under arms the whole time, and when at last the Emperor, convinced he must fly or be burned alive, consented to abandon the palace, it closed firmly around him, and passed into the tempest of fire. Over burning timbers, amid suffocating clouds of smoke and ashes, those bearskin caps were seen to move steadily as on the field of battle. Hither and thither the Conqueror of Europe turned in vain. Every way was blocked up by fire, and it was only at last by a postern gate that he could advance. But this, too, led into nothing but flame.

The streets became indistinguishable in the smoke and ruins. Only one winding street was left, and this seemed to pierce the ocean of fire rather than lead out of it. But Napoleon boldly entered it, while fragments of red hot iron roofs and burning timbers tumbling at his feet, and arresting his progress, and the crackling of flames and crash of falling houses, conspired to render the scene most appalling. At length the guide halted, not knowing whither to proceed. Here, probably, would have ended the history of Napoleon and his Old Guard, had it not been for some pillagers who happened to recognize the Emperor, and conducted him to a part of the town which had been burned to ashes in the morning, and thus left an open space where they could breathe again.

Still the danger was not over—to escape he was compelled to pass a long train of powder wagons that were slowly making their way out of the fire. When they at last reached the outskirts of the city, the Old Guard looked as if it had been in a hard fought battle. Their faces were blackened with smoke, their clothes and caps singed almost to a crisp, and the brave fellows themselves exhausted from being so long compelled to breathe heated air, smoke, and ashes. But calm, like their great leader, whom danger always tranquillized, they had met all with firm presence and unshaken courage.

After the destruction of the city, Napoleon returned to the Kremlin, which a battalion of the Guard had succeeded in saving. Here he continued to linger—almost every day reviewing his Guard— until a month had passed away, and the last of October, with its wintry premonitions, had come.

At length, however, he awoke from his strange infatuation, and commenced his retreat. From that moment his Guard became his stay, and ultimately his salvation.

An incident occurred during the conflagration, which illustrates the moral character of the Old Guard. Bouvier-Destouches, a lieutenant of the mounted grenadiers, had been able with some of his squadron, to save a part of the wealth of Prince Gagarin, when his palace was enveloped in flames. As a token of gratitude, the prince offered him a wooden dish full of vessels of gold, telling him to bury them till the fire was over, and then he could carry them away.

The Lieutenant thanked him, but refused the present, saying, "when one has the honor to belong to the Old Guard, the only recompense which can please him is the consciousness of having done his duty." The prince still urging his acceptance of the gift, the officer took the vessels, and hurling them through a window of the palace into the river, said gaily, "Prince, mark the spot where they fall, and when order is re-established, you can fish them up again." Strict honesty was one of the leading characteristics of the Old Guard. General Dorsenne, who commanded a corps of grenadiers, once said, "If I had a wagon load of gold, I would put it in the mess-room of my grenadiers—it would be safer there than under lock and key." During the retreat, as the army approached the

Beresina, the paymaster of the Guard fearing the chest would fall into the hands of the Cossacks, distributed the whole amount among the soldiers of the Guard, who put it in their knapsacks. When the army reached the other side of the river, it was rendered up again, and the amount, 2,000,000 of francs, found entire, with the exception of some two hundred francs, which had sunk with the grenadier who carried it in the waves of the Beresina.

CHAPTER 9

1812: the Old Guard in Russia

As I mentioned at the close of the last chapter, the moment Napoleon commenced his disastrous retreat, the Old Guard became his chief reliance. Not only was the discipline of the soldiers so perfect that no disorder of the army of the line could affect it, their courage so lofty that overwhelming numbers of the enemy, storms, frost, and famine, could not shake it, but the moral character they possessed was a guarantee against all plunder, misrule, and desertion. Amid the motley crowd laden with booty that passed from the gates of Moscow, the firm array and noble bearing of that Guard gave a prestige of its future conduct. Two thousand miles lay between those brave men and Paris—it mattered not, closing around their beloved chieftain, they were prepared for any fate that might befal. A few battalions were left behind, under Mortier, to blow up the Kremlin, who, after fighting four days with a hundred and eighty thousand pounds of powder under their feet, set fire to it, and then joined the main body.

A few days after the evacuation of Moscow, Napoleon narrowly escaped being made prisoner by the Cossacks. He had started early in the morning on the Kaluga road with only a few officers, leaving the four squadrons of the Guard, his regular escort, to overtake him. Before they arrived, as he was passing along without dreaming of immediate danger, he suddenly saw the crowds of men and women who filled the road in advance with vehicles, hurrying back in terror, overturning the wagons and creating a scene of indescribable confusion. Supposing it a groundless panic, he continued to move forward. At length the long black lines which had remained motionless in the distance, began to advance, and a moment after, six thousand Cossacks came dashing down in a wild gallop. Rapp cried out to the emperor, "It is the Cossacks, turn back." The latter disbelieving it, or too proud to fly, stood still. The furious hordes were already surrounding him, when Rapp seized the bridle of his horse, and turning him round, exclaimed, "Indeed you must turn back." Napoleon perceiving at length the full extent of his danger, immediately drew his sword and placing himself with Berthier and Caulincourt on the side of the road, calmly waited the attack of the barbarians. They approached to within fifty paces when Rapp flung himself on the foremost. A lance pierced his horse, and he fell. The aides-de-camp and a few horsemen of the Guard, extricated him. A moment after, however, Bessieres came thundering up with the cavalry of the Guard, and swept the field.

Soon after, winter began to set in, and the snow covering up concealed ditches and morasses, made such uncertain footing for the soldiers and unsafe ground for horses and artillery, that the loss of the army became immense. Over the field of Borodino laden with thirty thousand skeletons and wrecks of every description, through desolated provinces, living often on half raw horse flesh and rye water, the Old Guard, firm and uncomplaining, bore its emperor on till at last they approached Smolensko, the place where all their sorrows were to end, and plenty to be exchanged for famine, and warm bivouacks take the place of beds of snow and ice. The soldiers could not resist the alluring prospect, and broke their ranks and hurried forward, pell- mell towards the city. The commands of the officers were disregarded, even threats of punishment produced no effect. Food, and fire, and clothing, and rest, were before them. The gnawings of hunger, pinching frost, and starvation impelled them on, and they swept in one vast crowd to the gates. The Old Guard alone showed no symptoms of disorganization. Half naked, and cold, and hungry, they also were, but with steady step and unalterable mien, they continued their march in as perfect order as when they first crossed the Niemen.

The French troops in possession of Smolensko, saw this multitude of more than fifty thousand men approaching with haggard looks and wild cries, and fearing that such an irruption would end in a general pillage, and also to show that the desertion of their colors should never be rewarded, sternly shut the gates upon them. Then arose the most doleful cries, prayers and entreaties were mingled with threats and curses, and mass after mass precipitated itself against the gates to burst them open. Entreaties and violence were alike in vain, and many fell down dead from exhaustion.

Several hours after, the Guard came up, its ranks unbroken, its eagles above them; and moving steadily into the clamorous and excited throng, cleared a path for themselves to the gates. Their entrance guaranteed the safety of the city. The poor wretches pressed after, cursing the Guard, demanding if they were always to be a "privileged class, fellows kept for mere parade, who were never foremost but at reviews, festivities, and distributions, if the army was always to put up with their leavings." Despair and suffering had made them unjust.

Alas, this city which Napoleon supposed to be well supplied with provisions, proved barren as a desert. To their horror, instead of finding abundance to eat, the skeletons of horses, along the streets, from which the flesh had been peeled, showed that famine had been there before them. Around the scantily filled magazines the soldiers crowded with agonizing cries, and could scarcely be kept from murdering each other to get a morsel of food. But this dreadful example had no effect on the Guard. They knew that more than a month of toil and suffering, of combats with the cold and the enemy, must be endured, before they could reach a place of safety— yet the same severity and order marked all their conduct.

After remaining here five days, Napoleon issued orders to re-commence the retreat. The debris of the cavalry had been collected together, the half-destroyed battalions united into separate corps, while eight or nine thousand infantry, and some two thousand cavalry of the Guard, all that remained, were put in the best conditions their straitened circumstances would permit—and on the 14th of November, at five o'clock in the morning, the whole marched out of Smolensko. Napoleon, with the Guard in a solid column, was in advance. Its march was firm as ever, but gloomy as the grave. Daylight had not yet appeared, and that dark column passed out upon the snow fields, silent as death. Not a drum or a bugle cheered their march, and more sombre and sterner than all, rode Napoleon in their midst, his great soul wrung with silent agony. The cracking of whips as the drivers lashed their horses, or a smothered imprecation as horses, and men, and cannon rolled down a declivity in the darkness together, were the only sounds that broke the stillness of the morning, as the doomed host lost itself in the deepening gloom of a northern winter. It made but thirteen miles the first day, a distance it took the artillery of the Guard twenty-two hours to accomplish. Such was the first day's march, making scarce a mile an hour through the snow and frost, yet it was the easiest they were to have for a month to come.

While the imperial column was thus toiling forward, the enemy had got in advance and occupied the road between it and Krasnoi with a battery and thirty squadrons of horse. The leading corps of the French army was thrown into disorder by this sudden appearance of the enemy, and would have broken and fled, but for a wounded officer, the brave Excelmans, who, although having no command, immediately assumed it in the face of the proper leader, and by his energy and daring, restored order. He thus succeeded in putting on a bold front which intimidated the squadrons, and they dared not charge. The battery, however, kept up an incessant fire, the balls at every discharge crossing the road along which the column was marching. When it came the turn of the Old Guard to pass, they closed their ranks in a solid wall of flesh around the emperor, and moved steadily into the fire, while their band of music struck up the air, "Où peut-on être mieux qu' au sein de sa famille?" "Where can one be happier than in the bosom of his family?" Napoleon stopped them, exclaiming, "Play rather Veillons au salut de l'Empire." "Let us watch for the safety of the Empire.

As soon as the Old Guard had passed, the Russian commander, who had not dared even with his vastly superior force to arrest this terrible corps, threw twenty thousand men across the road on all the heights around, thus dividing Napoleon from Eugene, Davoust, and Ney, who were bringing up the rear. Mortier had escaped, but Eugene was compelled to fight his way through, with the loss of nearly his whole division. Davoust was next in rear. Ney came last, though no news had been received from him for a long time.

Although at Krasnoi Napoleon saw the enemy in immense force surrounding him to take him prisoner, he would not leave the place till assured of the safety of his lieutenants. He had heard all day long the cannonading which annihilated Eugene's corps, but could not succor him.

After the prince had escaped, his anxiety for Davoust and Ney was redoubled. He had determined, before the arrival of Eugene, to face about, and with his feeble force attack the enemy, and thus make a great effort, but a still greater sacrifice for those noble officers. Still holding to this determination, he sent forward Eugene with the miserable wreck of his corps, while he, with his Old Guard, prepared to march back on the Russian army, and attempt to save Davoust and Ney. The night before, however, the Young Guard, under Roquet, crushed to atoms a vanguard of Russian infantry, which had taken position in front of Napoleon, to cut off his retreat. The latter ordered him to attack the enemy in the dark, and with the bayonet alone, saying that this was "the first time he had exhibited so much audacity, and he would make him repent it in such a way that he should never again dare approach so near his headquarters." The complete success of the expedition detained the Russian army twenty-four hours—a delay of vast importance to the French.

In the morning, before daylight, Napoleon placed himself on foot in the midst of the Old Guard and issued from Krasnoi. As he grasped his sword, he said, "I have sufficiently acted the Emperor—it is time I became the General." Perhaps there is not a more sublime exhibition of heroism in the whole of his career than this effort to save Davoust and Ney. With only six thousand of his Guard, and some five thousand under Mortier, composed chiefly of the Young Guard, he turned to meet eighty thousand victorious troops, entrenched on commanding heights and protected by a powerful artillery. The enemy was sweeping round him in a vast semi-circle and a few hours of delay might cut off his retreat entirely, yet he resolved to march back instead of forward, and to lessen his force in a hopeless combat, instead of preserving it for his own use. He well knew the peril of the undertaking, but he had determined to succor his brave marshals or perish in the attempt.

Silently and sternly this brave band retraced its steps over the snow-covered field, uttering no complaint, and ready as ever to be sacrificed at the will of their beloved leader. When daylight dawned, lo, on three sides of them the Russian batteries crowned the heights. Into the "centre of that terrible circle" the old Guard moved with an intrepid step and took up its position. A few yards in advance, Mortier deployed his five thousand in front of the whole army, and the battle opened, if that can be called a battle in which a small devoted band stands and is shot down, solely to attract the enemy's force from another quarter. The Russians needed only to advance, and by the mere weight of its masses, crush that Old Guard to atoms. But awed by its firm presence, and more than all by the terrible renown it had won, and by the still greater renown of its leader whom they regarded almost as a supernatural being, they dared not close with it. They, however, trained their cannon on the ranks, through which the shot went tearing with frightful effect—but without a movement of impatience, the living closed over the dead to be trodden under foot in turn. Thus girdled with fire, they stood hour after hour, while Napoleon strained his eager gaze to catch a glimpse of Davoust and Ney. At length he saw Davoust alone, dragging his weary columns through clouds of Cossacks and marching straight on the Russian batteries. But as the soldiers came in sight of Krasnoi, they disbanded, and making a detour to escape the enemy's guns, rushed pell-mell into the place.

Napoleon having seen half his Guard shot down, commenced his retreat, leaving Mortier with the Young Guard to keep the enemy in check as long as he could, telling

The Russian Campaign

him that he would send back Davoust with his rallied troops to his assistance. They must, if possible, hold out till night and then rejoin him. The enemy he said was overwhelming him on every side, and soon his retreat would be entirely cut off and he must push on and occupy the passage of the Borysthenes, or all would be lost. He pressed this brave marshal's hand sorrowfully as he parted from him, and traversing Krasnoi, cleared the road beyond it as he advanced. But Mortier could not obey the orders he had received, for a part of the Young Guard had lost an important post they had been defending, and the Russians emboldened by Napoleon's departure, began to close slowly around him. Roquet endeavored to take the position that had been lost, and from which a Russian battery was now vomiting death on its ranks, but of the regiment which he sent against it, only eleven officers and fifty soldiers returned to tell how they fought and fell. It was then that Mortier performed that admirable movement which shed such glory on him and the Young Guard. With the three thousand, all that was left of his five thousand, he wheeled and marched in ordinary time out of that concentrated fire.

Ney was left behind abandoned of all, and apparently a doomed man, yet to exhibit still greater heroism, and furnish a still more miraculous page in the history of this unparalleled retreat.

Napoleon continuing his retreat, came to Dombrowna, a town built of wood, where he encamped for the night, and obtained some provisions. In the night he was heard groaning—the name of Ney ever and anon escaping his lips—and mourning over the sufferings of his poor soldiers, and yet declaring that it was impossible to help them without stopping, and this he could not do with no ammunition, provisions, or artillery. He had not force enough to make a halt. "He must reach Minsk as quickly as possible." Here were his magazines, his great hope, towards which he was toiling with the energy of despair.

But scarcely had these words escaped him, when a Polish officer arrived, stating that Minsk had been taken by the enemy. Napoleon was struck dumb by this new and overwhelming disaster; then raising his head, he said, "Well, there is nothing left now, but to clear our passage with our bayonets."

Despatches were immediately sent to the different portions of the army in advance, where they had remained during the march of the grand army to Moscow; and then, dejected and worn out, he sunk into a lethargy. It was not yet daylight when a sudden tumult aroused him from his stupor. He sent Rapp out to ascertain the cause. But the uproar increasing, he imagined that a nocturnal attack had been made upon his head-quarters, and immediately inquired if the artillery had been placed behind a ravine made by a stream that ran through the town. Being told that it had not, he hastened thither himself and saw it brought over. He then came back to his Old Guard who were standing to arms, and addressing each battalion in turn, said, "Grenadiers, we are retreating without being conquered by the enemy; let us not be vanquished by ourselves! Set an example to the army. Several of you have already deserted your eagles, and even thrown away your arms. I have no wish to have recourse to military laws to put a stop to this disorder, but appeal entirely to your sense of duty. Do justice to yourselves. To your own honor I commit the maintenance of your discipline."

This was all that was needed to make the grenadiers firm as iron. In fact it was rather whipping the other troops over the Old Guard's shoulders, for amid the general panic that prevailed in the darkness, when all believed the enemy was upon them, Napoleon on his return, found them standing in perfect order, and ready to charge on ten or ten thousand alike.

It proved a false alarm; order was restored, but only to be lost again a few hours after, among all but the Guard and a few hundred men belonging to Prince Eugene. The confused mass streamed along the road towards Orcha, the Guard alone showing the array of disciplined troops.

Six thousand were all that entered the place, out of that magnificent and veteran corps. Here the dangers thick-ened; for two armies were cutting off their retreat, while the winter was deepening, and the cold becoming more and more intense. There was nothing before the fragments of the grand army, but deserts of snow and ice over whose desolate bosom Cossacks were streaming, and the artillery of the enemy thundering. Napoleon resorted to threats to maintain discipline among his troops, but they had lost all fear of death—it was the slow torture that made them wild with despair. Nothing but the firm presence of the Old Guard and Eugene's few men prevented them from pil-laging Orcha, although situated on a friendly frontier. The wonder is not that soldiers under such sufferings should become disorganized, but that the few thousand of the Old Guard could resist the infectious example, especially as by their orderly march they lost all the provisions by day and fuel by night, which the stragglers were able to pick up; and suffered dreadfully the want of both. Minsk, beyond the Beresina, had kept alive their hopes, but now nothing but frozen deserts lay beyond that inhospitable river.

Still they stood firm. Napoleon had said to them, "Gren-adiers of my Guard, you are witnesses of the disorganiza-tion of the army. The greater part of your brethren have, by a deplorable fatality, thrown away their arms. If you imitate this sad example, all hope will be lost. The safety of the army is confided to you. You will justify the good opinion I have had of you. It is necessary not only that the officers among you maintain a severe discipline, but also that the soldiers should exercise a rigorous surveillance, and themselves punish those who attempt to leave their ranks."

THE GUARD IN RUSSIA

This appeal to their honor was received in dead silence—not in words but in deeds they were to prove his confidence well placed; and shivering with cold and reeling from exhaustion, they closed sternly around him.

On the 20th of November, Napoleon quitted Orcha with his Guard, leaving behind him Eugene, Mortier, and Davoust to wait for Ney. The officers declared it was impossible that he should escape, but the emperor would not abandon the last hope. He knew the indomitable character of the man, and that he would perform everything short of miracles before he would surrender.

Four days after he heard that the heroic marshal was safe. When the courier brought the news he leaped into the air and shouted for joy, it was a sudden flash of light and hope on the night of his darkness and dejection.

But the horrors of this march increased as he advanced towards the Beresina, and when he arrived near that fatal river, he ordered all his eagles to be burned, together with half the wagons and carriages of the army, and the horses to be given to the artillery of the Guard. He commanded them also to lay hands on all the draught cattle within their reach, not sparing even his own horses, rather than leave a single cannon or ammunition wagon behind. Eighteen hundred dismounted cavalry of the Guard were rallied into two battalions, although but eleven hundred of them could be supplied with muskets or carbines. All the officers of the cavalry of the army that still had horses, formed themselves into a "sacred squadron" for the protection of the person of the emperor; and with this and the Old Guard as a fixed and central orb to retain the vast and straggling multitude—Napoleon, with a sack of poison on his breast to take in the last extremity rather than fall into the hands of the Cossacks, plunged into the gloomy forest of Minsk, and pressed forward to the desperate conflict that awaited him on the banks of the Beresina. Amid the double darkness of the night and the forest, thousands perished, and Napoleon with knit brow and compressed lip saw men in raging delirium constantly falling at his feet wildly entreating for help.

The frightful disorder that arose among the multitude during the awful passage of the Beresina, when the Old Guard at last began to cross, shows with what feelings the army regarded it. It was compelled to clear a passage for the emperor with the bayonet, though one corps of grenadiers, out of mere compassion, refused to exercise force on the despairing, pleading wretches, even to save themselves.

Having reached the opposite banks, they defended them during the succeeding days of storm, and battle, and death that marked the passage. It encamped near the ruins of Brelowa, in the open fields with Napoleon, also unsheltered, in their midst. During the day they were drawn up in order of battle, while the driving snow covered them as with a shroud; at night they bivouacked in a square around their suffering, yet intrepid leader. These veterans of a hundred battles would sit on their knapsacks feeding their feeble fires, their elbows planted on their knees, and their heads resting on their hands, doubling themselves up for the twofold purpose of retaining the little warmth they possessed, and of feeling less acutely the gnawings of empty stomachs. The nights were nearly sixteen hours long, and either filled with clouds of snow, or so piercing cold that the thermometer sunk to twenty, and sometimes to over thirty degrees below zero. Painful marches, fierce battles, tattered clothing, cold, and famine combined, were too much for human endurance, and in a few days one third of the Guard perished.

One who had seen that corps, on a review day in Paris, would not have recognized its uniform in the tattered vestments that half protected their persons. But they never murmured, never broke their solid formation, but clenching firmly with frozen fingers their muskets, struggled and died at their posts.

The following solitary incident illustrates the character and suffering of all. One day a mounted grenadier, or one who belonged to the corps of mounted grenadiers, though no longer possessing a horse, approached a fire occupied by various soldiers of the army. He was a tall, elegantly formed man, with a face full of serenity and firmness. He was covered with tatters of every color, having saved nothing of his handsome uniform but his sabre and a few pieces of the fur of his bear-skin cap, which he had wrapped around his head to protect it from the frost. His breath had congealed into icicles which hung from his lips and beard. He had but one boot, the other foot being enveloped in shreds of coarse cloth. As he approached the fire, he unrolled a small piece of linen cloth and held it out to dry, saying, "I will finish my washing." When it was dry he rolled a little tobacco in it, and said gaily "We are used up, but it is all the same, *Vive l' Empereur.* We have always thoroughly flogged these Russians, who are nothing but schoolboys compared to us."

Such was the destitution and such the spirit of this glorious old corps. It seems fabulous that any body of men could be subjected to the extremes of cold and hunger they underwent, and one be left alive to tell the tale of their sufferings and courage. Ever since they left Smolensko they had lived on horse flesh half roasted and rye water which in the absence of salt they seasoned with gunpowder.

From the Beresina to Smorgoni, the grand army exhibited nothing but a disordered mob, with the exception of the Guard. At the latter place Napoleon gave a farewell and agonized look upon it, and set out for Paris. Murat was left in command, but the giant mind had gone, and the Old Guard, scorning to take in its keeping an inferior person, voluntarily broke its ranks, and dispersed with the other stragglers. Its solid squares were no longer seen at night, nor its firm array by day, the trust and hope of all. The disorder then became frightful, and the last remaining days of the grand army presented the accumulation of all horrors.

The Guard still numbering three thousand men partook of these horrors and sufferings. The weather suddenly became intensely cold, the thermometer standing day after day from twenty to thirty degrees below zero. Floundering through snow drifts, piercing dark forests, the frozen multitude dragged itself along, the silence broken only by the crackling of ice under their feet, or the low moan or shriek of despair, or last faint cry of soldiers as they fell stiff and stark on the icy earth. The living trod over the dead without turning aside to avoid the corpses. They stopped only to take the last morsel of food f'rom the dying, and to pounce like wolves upon a fallen horse, and quarrel over his emaciated carcass.

The exhausted wretches strained their bloody eyes on the pitiless heavens, and then with heart-rending sighs, fell to rise no more. At night the strongest cut down fir trees for fire, into which the frozen stragglers as they arrived would often throw themselves, and be burned to a cinder. The frost seemed to attack the brains of many, causing the most frightful delirium. But the details are too horrible—let them rest with the dead who fattened with their corpses the deserts of Russia.

When the army arrived at Wilna, only a few platoons of the Old Guard remained, and they no longer obeyed the beat of the generale. Murat's shameful desertion of the army here completed the wreck.

The remains of that splendid army which in June had crossed the Niemen 500,000 strong, was now chased back by a detachment of cavalry. The solid squares of the Old Guard remained in Russia. Many of their bivouacs could be traced in the spring by the circle of skeletons that encompassed a heap of ashes. That "column of granite" had melted away, and nothing but its base was left on which another was to be speedily reared.

But its fame lasts. The courage that nothing could daunt the patient endurance under unheard of horrors, the sublime moral elevation of its character, its steadfast devotion to duty amid universal disorder, and which no bad example nor the last pangs of mortal agony could demoralize its lofty sense of honor triumphing over famine and death, will claim the admiration of the world till the end of time.

CHAPTER 10

1813

The Russian Campaign had swallowed up the French army, and Prussia immediately took up arms with Russia to complete the destruction of Napoleon. False and treacherous, the former deemed that now was the time to strike her unfortunate ally. But this lofty intellect and unconquerable will scorned to yield to the storm that was about to burst upon him in his helpless state. He looked around him and saw only the broken fragments of an army. The Old Guard, with its artillery and cavalry, was gone. Still there was a nucleus left. He had but eight hundred at Marengo, and yet he made it terrible to the enemy. It is true he was without cannon—nearly a thousand were strewed by the way in his retreat from Russia—he had no trained horses, they had died or been eaten for food, and there were disciplined and strong armies, well supplied both with artillery and cavalry, to be met. Already they were marching on the possessions of France.

Yet from this desolation, Napoleon determined to create an army with both artillery and cavalry, and roll back the presumptuous enemy who dared to menace the soil of France, and assail his throne. Four veteran regiments of the Old Guard remained in Spain—these were recalled. Cannon from the arsenals, and artillerists from the ships of war were collected, horses purchased, and a conscription set on foot, which soon brought to his standard a vast army. But such had been the drain on France to support the former wars, that the conscription descended to mere youths, seventeen years old, and the pupils of the Guard were brought forward. The National Guard of France, a hundred thousand well disciplined men, were also incorporated into the army, while the Guards of Honor, as they were called, composed of the sons of wealthy and distinguished families, recruited the cavalry. The guards of honor were mounted bodies of men in the various cities of France—organized merely to receive and attend Napoleon when he passed through their respective places, and were wholly unfit for service. The élite of the army of the line were taken to compose the Old Guard, and it soon assumed its former appearance.

The greatest enthusiasm prevailed among the soldiers, and soon this new army took up its line of march for Germany, to join the relics of the different corps that still remained there after the retreat from Russia. Although deficient in cavalry, Napoleon immediately assumed the offensive, and pressed forward to seek the allies near Leipzic. Poserna, on the way to Lutzen, was defended, and in taking those heights, Bessieres, the commander of the Old Guard, was struck dead by a cannon-ball. This brave officer, who had risen from the ranks to Marshal of the empire, was dearly loved by the Guard. When it was composed of but eight hundred men, and laid the foundation of its fame at Marengo, he was at the head of it. Through all the terrible campaigns of Napoleon in Italy and Spain, at Austerlitz, Wagram, and Eylau, through all the disastrous retreat from Russia, he had headed its invincible columns. Noble in heart, heroic in courage, of great integrity of character, his death was an irreparable loss to the Emperor

LEIPZIG

and to the Guard. His body was embalmed, and sent to the Hotel des Invalides.

That night Napoleon encamped in the plain where rose the tomb of Gustavus Adolphus. The next day the battle of Lutzen was fought. Early in the morning the heavy cannonading on the right, where Ney commanded, showed that there was to be the weight of the battle. In a short time, the concentration of heavy masses in that part of the field by the enemy, had driven back the French a mile and a half. The five villages, which formed their stronghold, were all carried, after having been taken and retaken several times. Ney had exhibited his old valor, and the young conscripts under him, who then for the first time were under fire, behaved like veterans. "Five times," said he, 'I led back those brave youths to the charge." But their valor was vain, and the victorious enemy was pushing them fiercely from their positions.

When the news of this disaster reached Napoleon, he turned to Berthier and Caulincourt, with the exclamation "Ha!" accompanied by a look which "froze every heart around him with horror." The day was wellneigh lost, and he knew it. But instead of yielding to discouragement, he rose with the increasing danger, and set off on a gallop, followed by his invincible Guard, to the scene of disaster.

Where the cannonading was heaviest, and the clouds of smoke rose thickest, thither he directed his course. The field was covered with fugitives; while the columns that were still unbroken, were slowly retiring. Clouds of the enemy's cavalry were waiting impatiently till the last village was cleared and the retreating troops should deploy in the open plain, to sweep down on them, and complete their destruction.

But hope revived at Napoleon's presence—the conscripts rallied again, and shouts of *"Vive l'Empereur,"* rolled along the lines. Placing himself behind Ney's division, he rallied it, and sent it forward to the attack. Intrepidly advancing, it drove back the enemy, and retook a portion of the first village. But the allies receiving reinforcements, returned to the assault, and a bloody combat ensued around the shattered houses.

Neither party, however, could win the victory, but Napoleon gained what he stood in desperate need of —time for the foot soldiers and artillery of the Guard to arrive. Soon the bear-skin caps appeared, and infantry and artillery came thundering up to the Emperor, who had hardly time to form its massive columns of attack, when the French were again driven out of the village, while the shouts of the enemy were heard above the roar of the cannon. The Emperor threw one glance upon his flying troops, and then ordered Drouot, with sixty guns, to advance, and ten battalions of the Guard to follow. This dreadful artillerist cleared a way for his cannon through the crowd of fugitives that covered the plain, and opened his swift and deadly fire. Its effect was tremendous! To the distant observer the guns never seemed to stop, but to fire as they moved. Pressing steadily after, the Guard enveloped in smoke, pushed on, carrying village after village with loud hurrahs. In the close and deadly combat, officers were falling on every side, and the enemy struggled nobly to retain some portion of their conquests—flinging themselves, cavalry and infantry, in desperate valor, on those swiftly advancing columns. But onsets of cavalry, the fire of the artillery, were alike unheeded—in a solid mass those bear-skin caps were seen moving through the smoke, while the flash of their guns kept receding farther and farther, in the distance. Twilight gathered over the landscape, yet the outlines of that resistless column were revealed by the blaze of its guns, still advancing, till the field was swept and the victory gained.

Next morning the track of the Guard could he followed by the heaps of the dead it had left in its frightful passage.

The sight of the French conscripts who had fallen round those villages was mournful in the extreme. Mere youths—their forms not yet developed into manhood, their boyish features covered with blood, and stiffened in death—gave a still more horrid aspect to the field, and uttered a new malediction on war.

CHARACTER OF DROUOT

Drouot was perhaps the most remarkable artillerist the world has ever produced. He commanded the artillery of the Guard to the last, and made it the most terrible and deadly that ever swept a battle-field. Napoleon always kept him for great emergencies, and when this bold, stern man received an order in the midst of a battle to bring up his guns, he knew it was not to defend a point, but to recover a half-lost field, and move fiercely and steadily on victorious and overpowering troops. At such times he set off on a gallop, while the field shook under the weight of his cannon, as they came thundering after. He was perfectly aware of the dangerous position he held, and when about to advance on the enemy, he always dismounted, and placing himself on foot, in the midst of his guns, dressed in his old uniform of general of artillery, walked firmly into the hottest fire. He was somewhat superstitious about this uniform—he had never been wounded in it, and hence came to regard it as a sort of charm, or at least believed that good luck went with it; and strange to say in all the bloody and frightful combats he fought, neither he nor his horse was ever wounded. He always carried a Bible with him—it was on his person in battle, and the reading of it constituted his chief delight. He made no secret of this among the staff of the Emperor, which showed more courage than to face a battery. He knew everything belonging to his profession, and yet was modest as the most humble. His character seemed to be affected by the life he led, in a remarkable degree. Its solidity, the absence of all show and the presence of real strength, his quiet and grave demeanor, and the steadfastness of his affection and purpose, reminded one of the solidity and strength of his artillery.

In Napoleon's advance to Dresden, and passage of the Elbe at that place, an incident occurred that illustrates the characters of both. After bridges of rafts had been constructed, and a small portion of the troop got over during the night time, Napoleon saw fifty cannon of the enemy advance, and threaten a determined resistance to the passage. He immediately shouted to Drouot, "a hundred pieces of cannon!" The artillery of the Guard was hurried up, and Drouot posted them on the heights of Preisnitz. Napoleon, who was a little distance in the rear, was impatient, because the effect of the tire was not immediately visible, and reproached the former bitterly for not placing his pieces better, even pulling the old soldier's ears in his pet. Drouot calmly replied, "that the guns could not be better placed;" and so it proved, for under the tremendous fire which he kept up, the Russian batteries were soon silenced.

At the battle of Bautzen, which soon followed, Drouot's artillery scourged the enemy severely while the Old Guard itself sustained the grand attack in the centre, by which the victory was gained. Its squares surrounded the tent of Napoleon that evening, while its bands of music greeted him with victorious airs.

By daybreak next morning the pursuit was commenced, and pushed with the utmost fierceness. The allies had marched all night, but their rear-guard was soon overtaken, posted on strong heights, with forty pieces of cannon. Napoleon dared not attack it till the cavalry of the Guard should arrive. This body of men, six thousand strong, no sooner approached than it was put under Latour Maubourg, and advancing, overthrew the Russian cavalry in the plains, and rushing with loud shouts up the slopes of the heights, forced the enemy to retreat.

The defeated allies, however, retired in such good order, that no decisive blow could be struck and Napoleon, enraged to see a great victory turn out so barren of results, pushed forward with his escort to give greater energy to the attacks, and was still pressing on amid the cannon-balls that were whistling about him, when one of his escort was struck at his side. He turned to Duroc and said, "fortune is resolved to have one of us to-day"—prophetic words—a few moments after, as he was going along a narrow way, followed by his escort four abreast on a rapid trot, a cannon-ball struck a tree near him, glanced and killed Kugener, and mortally wounded Duroc. When this was announced to Napoleon, he dismounted, and gazed long and sternly on the battery from which the shot had been fired, then entered the cottage into which the Grand Marshal had been carried and where he lay dying.

This scene I have described in another work, but I will quote from that description the portion which illustrates the relation that existed between Napoleon and his Guard.

> After the last afflicting interview with the dying hero and friend, he ordered his tent to be pitched near the cottage where he lay, and entering it, passed the night all alone in inconsolable grief. The Old Guard formed their protecting squares about him, and the fierce tumult of battle gave way to one of the most touching scenes in history.
>
> Twilight was deepening over the field, and the heavy tread of the ranks going to their bivouacs, the low rumbling of artillery wagons in the distance,

and all the subdued sounds of a mighty host about sinking to repose rose on the evening air, imparting still greater solemnity to the hour. Napoleon with his grey coat wrapped about him, his elbows on his knees, and his forehead resting on his hands, sat apart from all, buried in the profoundest melancholy his most intimate friends dared not approach him, and his favorite officers stood in groups at a distance, gazing anxiously and sadly on that silent tent. But immense consequences were hanging on the movements of the next morning—a powerful enemy was near with its array yet unbroken—and they at length ventured to approach and ask for orders. But he only shook his head, exclaiming 'everything to-morrow;' and still kept his mournful attitude. No sobs escaped him, but silent and motionless he sat, his pallid face buried in his hands, and his great heart wrung with agony.

Darkness drew her curtain over the scene, and the stars came out one after another in the sky, and at length the moon rose over the hills, bathing in her soft beams the tented host, while the flames from burning villages in the distance, shed a lurid light through the gloom, and all was sad, mournful, and sublime. There was the dark cottage in which Duroc lay dying, with the sentinels at the door, and there, too, was the solitary tent of Napoleon. Around it at a distance, stood the squares of the Old Guard, and nearer by a silent group of chieftains, and over all lay the moonlight.

Those brave soldiers, filled with grief to see their beloved chief bowed down with such sorrow, stood for a long time tearful and silent, except as one would say to his comrade, 'Our poor Emperor has lost one of

LUTZEN

his children.' At length, to break the mournful silence, and to express the sympathy they might not speak, the bands struck up a requiem for the dying Marshal. The melancholy strains arose and fell in prolonged echoes over the field, and swept in softened cadences on the ear of the fainting warrior—but still Napoleon moved not. They then changed the measure to a triumphant strain, and the thrilling trumpets breathed forth their most joyful notes, till the night rung with the melody. With such bursts of music had they been used to welcome their chief after a day of battle and of victory, till his eye kindled in exultation—but now they fell on a dull and listless ear. It ceased, and again the mournful requiem filled the air. But nothing could arouse him from his agonizing reflections—his friend lay dying, and the heart he loved so dearly was throbbing its last pulsations.

This scene exhibits in a touching manner the sympathy that existed between Napoleon and his Guard,—and how heroically, yet how tenderly, was it here expressed. Enfolding him in their rock-fast squares, their hearts melted at the sorrow of him they protected, and the trumpets that but an hour before heralded their desperate charge strove to impart consolation by expressing the grief they dare utter in no other way. And then the thrilling blast upon blast, and loud exultant greeting, to rouse that overwhelmed heart from its stupor, and rekindle the emotions that were wont to sway it—how simple, yet how grand.

At length Napoleon entered Dresden, and an armistice was agreed upon. It ended, however, without any result, except to send Austria over to the side of the allies. Napoleon now had Russia, Prussia, Austria, Sweden, and Bohemia, combined against him, still he evinced no discouragement. Looking calmly around on the difficulties that environed him, he prepared to meet them with that genius and iron will before which the sovereigns who sought his life, had so often humbled themselves.

But prior to his departure from Dresden, he had a grand review of his army, which took place in a vast plain near the city. Accompanied by the King of Saxony and his suite and the Marshals of the Empire, he galloped the whole length of the line. As the Guard, twenty thousand strong, defiled before him, it seemed to carry the prestige of victory in its terrible standards. He then ordered a great banquet for the whole of the Guard.

At the commencement of hostilities, Marmont, Macdonald, and Ney, who were in Bohemia, were compelled to retire before the superior force of the enemy. When the news of the successive disasters of these marshals reached Napoleon, he took with him the Old Guard, and hastened to their relief. Infantry, cavalry, and artillery, went thundering through the Bohemian Mountains; and pouring like a torrent on the victorious enemy, rolled them back through the Silesian plains. In five days the Old Guard recovered all that had been lost.

But while the prospects were brightening around him in Bohemia, a dark and ominous storm was gathering over Dresden. St. Cyr with only thirty thousand men, had been left in possession of this city, against which the emperor believed no attack would be made. But suddenly a hundred and twenty thousand men and five hundred pieces of artillery darkened the heights around it. Couriers were hurriedly despatched to Napoleon, announcing the fact, who immediately put forth one of those prodigious efforts to save it, for which he was remarkable. He took with him his conquering Guard, and set out for the city. Although for four days it had marched on an average, twenty-five miles a day, fighting its passage besides, and slain six thousand men, it cheerfully turned its steps towards Dresden. Men gazed with astonishment on its swift movement. Although it was the month of August and the soldiers were worn out with their previous marches and combats, they swept forward with alacrity. Daybreak found them on the road, and night still in motion. Napoleon in their midst was devoured with the most painful anxiety. Knowing that the city could hold out but a short time against the overwhelming force gathered around it, he urged his faithful troops to their utmost speed. He wanted to give that Guard wings to transport it to Dresden. Breathless couriers dashing in one after another, telling him that if he did not arrive soon all would be lost, added to his impatience.

The troops had marched forty leagues in four days, and seemed about to break down. Napoleon saw that he had overtasked them, and fearing they would give out altogether, ordered twenty thousand bottles of wine to be distributed among them. Three thousand, however, were all that could be obtained. Refreshed by this scanty supply, they pressed forward, and at length from the heights that overlooked the city, gazed down on the thrilling spectacle. The two hosts were engaged, and the thunder of cannon rolled in heavy explosions over the hills. Columns of attack were already forming, and the innumerable array was swiftly closing around their comrades who were bravely bearing up against the shock. The Old Guard at once forgot their weariness at the sight—they saw their presence had never before been so urgently needed, and with proud hearts they thought how soon their eagles would be soaring over that tumultuous field, and their dread standards waving above a beaten foe. Like a resistless torrent they passed down the slopes and crowded swiftly forward over the bridges. The inhabitants, overjoyed at the sight of these renowned troops, rushed toward them with wine and bread—and though the wearied soldiers were parched with thirst, each and all refused the proffered refreshments, and marched steadily and swiftly on to the point of danger. They were soon standing side by side with their comrades who had combated so bravely, and with them breasting the tremendous storm of shells and shot that now deluged the city, they held that proud army in check till the arrival of the Young Guard.

The Old Guard entered the city at ten in the morning, and had fought all day with desperate valor to arrest the enemy, which, notwithstanding, made fearful progress. Some parts of the city were already inundated with their victorious troops; and at six o'clock, their cannon played within musket-shot of the walls. The arrival of the Young Guard at that hour drove the cloud from Napoleon's brow, and filled every heart with joy. He immediately ordered an attack. The gates were thrown open, and the Young Guard, under Ney, poured forth and rushing with loud cheers on the enemy, drove them back over the field. The Old Guard through another gate crushed everything in its passage, while Murat's splendid cavalry completed the discomfiture, and sent the astonished enemy back to the heights from which they had just descended in all the pride of victory, shouting, "to Paris, to Paris," as they came. The commanders who supposed the emperor was in Silesia, gazed with amazement at the Old Guard, and said one to another, "Napoleon is in Dresden."

The next morning at six o'clock. Napoleon was standing by a huge fire built in the squares of the Old Guard on the field they had won, while a cold and drizzling rain and mist darkened the ghastly scene. Behind, the cavalry of the Guard dismounted, stood beside their horses, ready at a moment's warning to dash to any part of the field.

Napoleon standing on that ploughed and dead-covered plain in the grey of the morning, in his plain overcoat, the steam arising like a cloud around his head as he dried himself beside the blazing fire, his hands crossed behind him, and his head bowed in deep thought, the Old Guard around him, the riders beside their steeds ready at a gesture to mount and charge— yet all quiet as a domestic scene not a muscle on that marble countenance rnoving, although the heavy roll of cannon from one end of the line to the other, announced that the work of death had commenced, presents one of the most striking and sublime spectacles in history.

In the battle that followed, Ney had command of the Young Guard, and again carried it in headlong valor on the enemy. It was a battery of the Guard that Napoleon, during the day, ordered to fire on a group which he took to be officers reconnoitring his position, and at the first discharge of which, Moreau fell.

The effects of this great victory, however, were lost by the almost simultaneous disasters that befel the divisions of Macdonald in Silesia, Oudinot at Gros Beeren, Marshal Ney at Dennewitz, and above all, of Vandamme at Toeplitz. Napoleon, with the Old Guard, could not be everywhere, and while with inferior force he was dealing terrible blows on portions of the allied army, his lieutenants lacking his genius, were defeated on every side. At this time too, Bavaria went over to the ranks of the allies. Napoleon, however, did all that man can do. With his tireless unconquerable Guard, he turned first on one side and then on the other, scattering the enemy from his path. But no sooner did he withdraw from the pursuit of one division to chastise another, than the former closed fiercely on his retiring columns. Thus in almost a circle of armies, he continued to battle bravely for victory, but at last was forced to retire to Leipsic, where, having concentrated his troops, he resolved to stake all on one great battle.

This was a hazardous move, for the allied powers could bring into the field nearly three hundred thousand men, and thirteen hundred cannon, while he had but a little more than half that force with which to meet them. The preparations for the battle were on the grandest scale, and when the two armies finally stood in array against each other, the most casual observer could see that the day foreboded a gloomy termination for Napoleon.

At midnight the night before, rockets sent up to an amazing height from the head- quarters of the allied army, and answered by others from Blucher on the north, told that all was ready; and early in the morning the earthquake commenced, and nearly two thousand cannon exploded on ranks of living men. Notwithstanding his inferiority of force, Napoleon's star seemed still in the ascendant, and his victorious eagles soared as of old over the smoke and tumult of the fight. Near the close of the day he deemed the victory secure, and ordered up the Young Guard, supported by the Old, to make his favorite attack on the centre, and finish the battle. The stern Drouot, with sixty cannon, moved in front, clearing a space for the column pressing after, and their advancing fire soon showed that the allied centre was shaken to its overthrow. The enemy seeing their centre in such extreme peril, brought up reserve after reserve, and battery after battery, and thousands of cavalry, and closed around those devoted troops. Yet the batteries of Drouot blazed on like a volcano. The heavy cuirassiers plunged boldly after, and the advance columns approached so far that they came near taking the Emperor Alexander and the king of Prussia prisoners, who were forced to mount and retire. But this invincible corps, after performing prodigies of valor, was at length compelled to halt, and night shut in the scene.

Napoleon pitched his tent in the bed of a dried fish-pond in the centre of the thinned squares of the Old Guard. The next day the battle opened gloomily for the French, for a hundred thousand fresh troops had joined the allies during the night, making an overwhelming preponderance of force. Still Napoleon showed a bold front, and strove with almost superhuman efforts to alter the decree written against him. Early in the day the brave Poniatowsky, after struggling nobly to retain his position, was finally driven back by superior numbers. Napoleon immediately hastened to the spot with two divisions of the Guard, and with one terrible blow stopped the advancing columns.

Soon after, news was brought that Victor and Lauriston, though fighting like lions, were on the point of being annihilated. With the two remaining divisions of the Guard he hastened to their relief. The field was covered with fugitives, and the scene of confusion that met his eye was enough to fill the boldest heart with dismay. But amid the thunder of artillery, the shouts of enraged men, and disorder around him, his brow bore a calm and serene aspect. Taking two battalions of the Guard, he cleared a path through the broken masses and hurled them with such awful violence on the advancing enemy, that they were broken in turn, and compelled to relinquish the ground they had so gallantly won.

The superiority of the allies could not make head against the obstinacy of Napoleon, for wherever the battle shook, there he plunged with his Guard and dealt such blows as it only could deal. But at this critical state of affairs still more alarming news was brought to him. His Saxon allies to the number of twelve thousand, with forty pieces of cannon, suddenly went over to the enemy. Thus not only in the crisis of the battle was the important point they held deserted, but a difference of twenty-four thousand men and eighty pieces of cannon, made to the French. Not content with their treason, no sooner did they reach the enemy's lines than they turned their batteries on the friends by whose side they had just stood.

It seemed as if fate having no compassion for his gallant bearing, was determined to push Napoleon to the verge of despair. The news of this defection startled him, for Schoenfield, lying close to the suburbs of Leipsic, was now threatened, and thus his whole line of retreat endangered. He instantly took a division of the Young Guard and Nansouty's cuirassiers and hastened to the spot, and arrested the further progress of the enemy—but he saw a retreat was inevitable.

I will not describe this horrible retreat, nor the appearance of a field on which a hundred and twenty thousand men had fallen. The Old and Young Guard had maintained their character on these two dreadful days, and its dead lay on every part of that field. The infantry were exposed throughout to the most tremendous fire. Its artillery, notwithstanding its numerical inferiority, was worked with terrible power, while the cavalry charged as only the cuirassiers of the Guard could charge—but its bravery and devotion only swelled the carnage—the defection of the Bavarians ruined every thing.

Battle of Hanau

Napoleon was now compelled to commence his disastrous retreat towards the Rhine. Outstripping his pursuers, he was approaching that river and the soil of France, when he received the astonishing news that General Wrede, his old ally, with fifty thousand Bavarians, had crossed his line of march and strongly posted at Hanau, was determined to finish the wreck of Leipsic. The French army, with the exception of the Guard, Old and Young, was a herd of stragglers. For nearly two hundred miles they had dragged their weary limbs towards the Rhine, harassed at every step by the Cossacks, and now, just as the soil of France was to welcome them, a fresh and powerful army unexpectedly crossed their path.

When this was told Napoleon, he simply said, "Advance; since these Bavarian gentlemen pretend to bar our passage, we must pass over their bellies." The Bavarians were posted in front of Hanau, stretching across the road, along which the French army was marching. Their centre was supported by seventy pieces of cannon, while between them and the approaching fugitives, stretched a forest several miles in extent. This was filled with sharp-shooters to retard the French, while the seventy cannon in battery were to receive them as they debouched on the farther side. Macdonald's and Victor's corps reduced to five thousand men, first entered the forest and cleared it, but the moment they attempted to form in the open field beyond, they were rent into fragments by the balls of those seventy guns, all trained on that devoted spot. Reinforcements kept arriving, but every effort was powerless to cross the plain in front of the forest. It was a wild hailstorm of balls in point-blank range, and the soldiers melted away before it like men of snow. It was then that Napoleon galloping up to his Guard ordered two battalions of foot chasseurs to clear the field, while at the same time he directed Drouot to advance with the artillery of the Guard.

"Remember," said he, "that on this very spot the French Guards under Louis XIV., were defeated and thrown into the river. Let the enemy to-day receive the same fate, and France be avenged."

For four hours Victor and Macdonald had vainly endeavored to bear up against the tremendous force that opposed them, and now the weary troops shouted for joy when they saw the bear skin caps of the old grenadiers enter the forest. Those black caps swept on like a wave through the green foliage—a line of flame marking their passage. As in the retreat from Moscow, no calamity however great, not even the pangs of famine, could shake their constancy—so now, after a weary flight of two hundred miles, they were the same as in the flush of victory.

The oaks rent round them before the cannon balls that crashed on every side—the huge limbs falling on their ranks, striking down many a brave man—but they pressed sternly on, cleared the wood, and soon won a part of the plain Victor and Macdonald had struggled for so many hours to obtain. In the open space they had thus snatched from the enemy, Drouot swiftly advanced with his trusty guns. At first with fifteen he opened his fire, then with fifteen rnore, then twenty, and so on till fifty played with all the rapidity and fearful accuracy which made the artillery of the Guard so formidable. He was in point-blank range, and the seventy pieces of the enemy gave them a superiority he must make up by rapidity of firing. It was terrific to see those hundred and twenty cannon concentrated on so narrow a space, and in such close range, exploding on each other. The guns of the Guard seemed to move in fire, so rapidly were they discharged, while the accuracy of aim soon told with fearful effect on the enemy.

In the midst of the volleys a large body of Bavarian cavalry suddenly precipitated themselves on the batteries of Drouot. The cannoneers seized their carbines—and now with the bayonet, and now with their pieces clubbed, stretched them around their guns. At this moment the cavalry of the Guard were seen debouching in dark and imposing masses from the forest. Wrede saw the gathering tempest that was about to burst upon him, and rallying his cavalry, and throwing his infantry into squares behind the

EYLAU

Russian dragoons, awaited the shock. The bugles sounded the charge and breaking into a trot, then into a gallop, those thundering squadrons fell on infantry, cavalry, and artillery with such resistless violence that the whole left wing of the army was swept from the plain. Wrede then threw forward his right and made a desperate effort to regain the ground he had lost. The troops advanced gallantly, and the artillery approached so near that the opposing gunners could hear each other's voices.

The scene then became indescribably fearful. It was one stream of lightning and peal of thunder through all the green alleys of the forest. The huge tops of the oaks swung to and fro and roared in the blast made by the balls as though a storm was sweeping over them. Giant branches were hurled through the air, and all amid the leafy recesses were seen charging columns and exploding batteries, and crowds of carriages and wagons, and a multitude of fugitives. In the centre of this forest was Napoleon walking to and fro in the road, listening with the deepest anxiety to the uproar around him, and conversing at intervals with Caulincourt. Defeat here he knew would be irretrievable ruin, for he would be driven back upon his pursuers, and crushed between two armies. While such painful thoughts were crowding his bosom a bomb fell in the ditch beside him, the fuse still burning. He paid no attention to it, and Caulincourt placing himself between it and the emperor, they continued their conversation as before. The officers of his staff looked on in amazement and held their breath in terror, but the shell had sunk so deep in the mire that it was extinguished before it had time to burst.

The firing in the forest becoming still heavier, Napoleon ordered two battalions of the Old Guard to advance, which charging almost on a run, overthrew everything in their passage, and forced the enemy into a precipitate retreat. This brave corps never behaved with greater intrepidity. A Captain Godau, at the head of only two companies, charged and overthrew several battalions of the Bavarians. Two chasseurs threw themselves in the tumult on the ranks of the enemy, and bore away each a standard. General Cambronne spurred all alone like Murat into the midst of the fray. Three soldiers seeing him dash forward, rushed after him—one of them snatching the banner of a guide from the very heart of a Bavarian battalion. The gunners fought with unparalleled heroism, and this "Column of granite" again showed itself worthy of the name it bore. It alone opened the road to the army, and saved it from utter annihilation.

That night, by the side of a blazing fire, in the heart of the forest, Napoleon bivouacked in the midst of his exhausted squares. He said afterwards that at Hanau he had not merely won a victory, but had carried a breach.

In this battle Wrede lost a fifth of his army, and Europe learned for the hundredth time the danger of attempting to stop the advance of the adamantine columns of the Old Guard.

With saddened hearts they defiled over the Rhine, and bid a final adieu to the scene of their achievements. Behind them lay Jena, Austerlitz, Wagram, Eylau, and a host of fields where their iron ranks had borne down everything that opposed them and their eagles soared in triumph—never to be revisited. On the soil of beloved France— by their own hearthstones they were now to show to the world examples of heroism unequalled in the annals of war.

Napoleon returned to Paris with a part of the Guard, to prepare for the inundation of his empire by nearly a million of men.

CHAPTER 11

1814: Campaign of the Guard

At the close of the year 1813, Napoleon presented a sad yet sublime spectacle. His first words on entering the senate, after his return from the disasters of Leipsic, were, "A year ago all Europe marched with us—to-day all Europe marches against us." From the vast height of power to which he had reached, he had descended step by step, battling bravely as he went. Deserted by his allies, betrayed by the men he had covered with honor, his dominions wrested one by one from his grasp, his brothers dethroned, and his own brother-in-law openly proclaiming his treason, some of the heaviest blows he received coming from the hands of those whose fortunes he had made, his army in fragments, his treasury exhausted, while the bayonets of nearly a million of men were pointing towards Paris, he yet showed no discouragement, uttered no complaints, but calm and resolute stood and surveyed the vast and dismaying prospect as he was wont to do a doubtful battle-field. He was grander in his great misfortunes than when with Europe pressing after his standard, he two years before crossed the Niemen in all the pomp and pride of a conqueror.

To replenish the treasury, to create an army, to awe the turbulent, and then stand up single-handed against Europe in arms—these were the tasks before him. He set the first example of self-sacrifice, by giving into the public treasury six millions of dollars taken from his private vaults in the Tuileries.

A decree ordering a levy of 300,000 soldiers was made, and another augmenting the Guard to 112,500 men. During January of this year he issued no less than five decrees concerning his Guard. He seemed to be more solicitous about it than ever before. In the disasters of the last two years he had felt its value more than in the full tide of victory. He had fallen back on it again and again in the hour of utmost peril, and always found it a "column of granite." Though its charge on the enemy's centre at Leipsic was not successful as at Wagram and other fields of its fame, yet it never made a nobler charge or showed more dauntless bravery. Treason and overwhelming numbers wrested the victory from its eagles.

The levy, however, was not successful. France was exhausted not only of her men, but even of her youth, and boys were now in his greatest need to form his battalions. To add to his trouble, as fortune always seems to delight in pushing down a falling favorite, the Typhus fever broke out among his troops along the Rhine. They had caught it in the plains of Germany, and these veterans who had fallen back from the different fortresses and cities which they held were swept off by thousands.

Thus he was deprived of a large number of the few experienced soldiers the disasters of the last year had left him. Notwithstanding all this and the appalling aspect of a million of men rising up and swearing to complete his overthrow—seven hundred thousand of them sweeping steadily down upon the soil of France, their bayonets pointing towards his capital—he stood nobly at bay. Having entrusted his wife and son to the National Guard in a speech full of feeling, he bade them adieu, little dreaming it was to be a final one, and set out for head-quarters at Chalons.

It was in the latter part of January that he reached the shattered and discouraged army, falling back on every side before the enemy. Rallying it by his presence, he immediately took the offensive and surprised Blucher with thirty thousand men near Brienne. The latter, however, made a stubborn resistance, and the advance guard of the French was forced to retire, when eight thousand of the Old Guard arrived and cleared the field. Blucher, however, rallied his troops behind his formidable artillery, and prepared to give battle on the following morning. Mortier who had made this bold irruption, fell back to wait the arrival of the main body, toiling up through mud and snow which the artillery sank at every step, made but slow progress. A Captain Hauillet, with a single company of the foot chasseurs of the Old Guard, was appointed to cover this retrograde movement. But soon after he had taken his position, an overwhelming force of Austrians suddenly came upon him. There seemed no escape to this devoted little band—but they were a part of the Old Guard, and if they fell, it would be like the Spartan band in Thermopylæ. Their heroic officer immediately concentrated his few soldiers and calling together the drummers he ordered the chasseurs not to fire, but to advance with the bayonet. The charge was then beaten and at the head of only a hundred and fifty men, he flung himself with such desperate energy on the five thousand Austrians advancing against him, that he broke their ranks in pieces, and put them to flight.

The battle of Brienne followed, and although the columns of the Old and Young Guard pressed forward amid the driving snow against the batteries, and stood firm under repeated charges of cavalry and infantry, yet they could not wring victory from the enemy. The constantly increasing forces of the allies rendered their numerical superiority so great that Napoleon at night ordered a retreat. He fell back to Troyes, and three days after to Nogent.

In the meantime the allied army divided. The Austrians following up Napoleon, were to march on Paris by way of Montereau down the valley of the Seine, while Blucher with the army of Silesia was to move upon Chalons, and descend by the Marne to the capital. The latter, full of energy and decision, was the antagonist first to be disposed of—for sweeping over the country without opposition, driving the affrighted peasants in crowds before him, he marched so rapidly towards Paris that the inhabitants were filled with terror.

Crippled for want of soldiers, Napoleon was unable to resist both of these formidable arrays at once, and resolved therefore to leave Victor and Oudinot with a small portion of the troops to check, as long as possible, the slow and methodical advance of the Austrians, and with the elite of the army, dash across country and inflict a sudden and terrible blow on Blucher. The latter knew that Napoleon was on his left, but this gave him no disquietude, for the head-quarters of the emperor were thirty miles distant, and the cross-roads were nothing but beds of mortar through which it would be impossible for him to drag his artillery. Besides, he had on his hands the allied army vastly superior to his own even undivided, and he would not dare leave it an open road to Paris. But a desperate condition requires desperate measures, and the advantage to Napoleon of the foolish dislocation of the invading army was too great to be neglected.

So on the 9th of February he started from Nogent, and at night was half way to Blucher. But such was the state of the roads, that it required the most extraordinary exertions to complete those fifteen miles. The artillery carriages rolled along up to their axles in mud, the cavalry floundered on, while the foot soldiers could scarcely force their way. Next morning, after entering the forest of Traconne the roads became still worse, the cannon stuck fast in the clay, and the drivers declaring it was impossible to extricate them, Marmont, who commanded the advance, wheeled about. When the state of things was reported to Napoleon, he said, "The passage must be made even though the cannon are left behind."

He would have been compelled to make this sacrifice of his guns, if the mayor of Barbonne had not at his command furnished five hundred horses, by which they were at length pulled out. Early on the morning of the 10th, the troops were all reunited, with the exception of a division of mounted grenadiers of the Guard which could not get through, the army in advance had so cut up and encumbered the road.

In the meantime Marmont heading still the advance, ascended at nine o'clock the heights that overlook the valley of Petit Morin, and saw with delight a corps of 5000 Prussians below him; the soldiers unconscious of danger, quietly preparing their breakfast. No sooner did the Emperor's eye take in the welcome spectacle, than he ordered a general attack, and a butchery and rout followed. The Prussian General with nearly the whole corps was taken. By this grand stroke he had cut the allied army in two, and could turn on whichever he liked.

The next morning at five o'clock, Napoleon was on horseback, hurrying on his weary troops to Montmirail to intercept Sacken, another of Blucher's generals, who, astounded at this sudden apparition of the French Emperor on his flanks, was making all haste to join his commander. But the Old Guard proved too quick for him, the infantry had left the field of battle where they had bivouacked an hour before daylight, and preceded by the mounted chasseurs, reached Montmirail, as Sacken was approaching it. The latter, to whom this town, lying as it did directly in his path, was of vital importance, immediately commenced an attack. Being superior in numbers, he was able to maintain the fight for five hours without losing ground. At length, as night approached, sixteen battalions of the Old Guard arrived, under Friant. These were immediately formed into a single column, each battalion a hundred steps from the other, and ordered to advance full on the enemy's centre.

At the same time Mortier arrived with sixteen other battalions of the Young Guard, six of which took their station on the right of Friant, to sustain the attacks of the Old Guard. Sacken had forty cannon placed so as to command the approaches to his central position, while a triple row of tirailleurs sustained by battalions of infantry, lined the hedges on either side.

On these murderous batteries and over these formidable obstacles the Old Guard led by Ney, advanced. Napoleon himself gave the signal of attack, and those resolute veterans charged on a run over the farm of Haute Epine. The combat was frightful— Sacken was fighting for life—Napoleon for his empire. The Prussians were determined to be cut down to a man rather than yield, and the Old Guard for once seemed to have charged a rock—but at this moment Napoleon ordered the lancers, dragoons, and mounted grenadiers, to gain the rear and fall suddenly on the shattered masses of the enemy.

As they defiled past him he said, "Brave young men, there is the enemy, will you allow him to march to Paris?"

Shaking their sabres above their heads, they exclaimed, "We will not," and rending the air with shouts, broke into a gallop, and falling with irresistible power on the hitherto steady ranks, trampled them under their horses' hoofs.

The rout was complete, and but the mere debris of the army escaped by a disorderly flight through the fields.

Night had now arrived, and Napoleon commanded the rally to be sounded in order to rest his exhausted troops for the next day's efforts. He slept in a farmhouse on some straw from which the enemy's wounded had just been removed, while four thousand men lay dead or dying around him. The next morning the reveille beat before daybreak, and Napoleon at the head of his tireless Guard started in pursuit. Eight Prussian battalions which did not arrive till too late to take part in the battle, covered Sacken's retreat. As the French approached, these battalions advanced to meet them, but a battalion of the Old Guard drove in the tirailleurs, while six other battalions fell on them in front. At the same time the dragoons of the Guard came thundering on, breaking through the first and second lines, and putting all to flight. The enemy lost two thousand more during the retreat of this day.

In the meantime, Blucher, who was at Virtus, had been informed of the sudden apparition of Napoleon among his divided corps by the disasters at Champ Aubert; and while the fugitives from that fatal field were pouring into the streets of the town where he lay, he heard the heavy cannonading at Montmirail and knew the danger in which Sacken was placed. Still he could not march to his relief, for he had but few troops with him, and Marmont was watching his movements. Besides he was waiting for the arrival of two corps, which were hastening to join him. At length being reinforced, he set out for Montmirail, driving Marmont before him.

Napoleon, as we have seen, had started on the 9th across the country, making thirty miles of horrible road by the morning of the 10th—having marched all night—the same day he gained the battle of Champ Aubert, the next, the

11th, he fought and won that of Montmirail, the 12th he kept up the pursuit, fighting as he went, and yet on the night of the 13th, hearing that Blucher had advanced to Etoges, he set out with his Guard and a portion of his other forces, and next morning was marching full on that place. Marmont had just evacuated the little village of Vaux Champ, fighting bravely as he retired, and was retreating along the road to Montmirail, when the bear-skin caps and eagles of the Old Guard suddenly appeared.

The effect was electric. The retreating troops halted, and rending the air with the most frantic hurrahs, demanded to be led against the enemy. The Emperor was in their midst, and amid the long and deafening shouts of "Vive l'Empereur," the cavalry went hurrying forward, while the skirmishers gave way to the heads of massive columns of infantry that went rolling on the foe. Marmont's squadron of escort charged alone on the Prussians. Four squadrons of service of Napoleon followed them. Soon the whole French line was in movement, and Blucher was compelled to retreat.

The road along which he passed was lined with lofty elms—in this he placed his artillery, which fired as it retired, while the infantry in solid squares moved through the fields on either side. On these the cavalry of the Guard charged incessantly, mowing them down with terrible slaughter. Especially when the enemy had passed Janvilliers and debouched into the vast open country beyond, the carnage became frightful.

Drouot with his artillery, strewed the plain with the dead, while the cavalry thundered on the shaking masses in repeated shocks, carrying away whole regiments at a time. But for the miry soil in which the horse artillery got fastened, Grouchy would have taken Blucher with his whole army. As it was, out of 90,000 men, he saved less than two thirds. The cavalry of the Guard was in constant action during this combat, and with Grouchy and his squadrons, covered itself with glory.

That night Napoleon, with the Old Guard, slept at Montmirail. But though the Guard had now travelled and fought six days without intermission, Napoleon started with it in the morning to the help of Victor and Oudinot, whom the allies, after his departure, had assailed and driven back almost to the gates of Paris.

It is painful to witness his gigantic efforts at this period, and remember they did not prove successful. After having by unheard of exertion carried his army and artillery across a country considered impassable, and fought and beaten a superior enemy five days in succession, he was overrun by couriers announcing to him that Nogent had been taken by assault, Moret, Nemours, and Montargis had fallen, that the advanced posts of the enemy were at the gates of Orleans, and the Cossacks were swarming through the forest and palace of Fontainbleau—that Auxerre had been captured and the garrison put to the sword, and the light troops of the enemy were covering the whole plain between the Seine and Loire, and that the reserve artillery and heavy baggage of the army had nearly reached the tages of Paris in its flight, filling the inhabitants with consternation. Such were the tidings that from hour to hour reached his ears, as he and his devoted Guard were pressing so fiercely the army of Blucher.

No wonder he could not rest. With one inferior army he must fight two, thirty or forty miles apart. Nothing but winged troops could do this long. Still his courage and will remained unshaken. Leaving Marmont, Mortier, and Grouchy, to watch Blucher, as he had left Victor and Oudinot to resist the advance of the allies, he took with him only his tireless Guard and the cuirasseurs, and started to the help of his hard pressed lieutenants. The roads were so bad that he could not go directly across the country, and he therefore turned aside and plunged into the forest of Brie, which he found filled with fugitives, fleeing before the enemy. The infantry went by post while the cavalry marched day and night for thirty-six hours. No troops but the unconquerable Guard could have undergone the exertions and labor they had endured for six days, and then made this cross march of thirty-six hours over almost impassable roads, for the sole purpose of attacking a fresh and superior enemy.

Such deeds as these elevate it above the common standard of mortals, and fill the mind with wonder and admiration.

It was high time for Bonaparte to arrive. He had sent a despatch to Victor and Oudinot announcing that he would come by the cross-road to Chalons, and they were straining every nerve to preserve it open, for if once closed by the enemy, it would be out of the power of Napoleon to effect a junction with them. As the post wagons and other vehicles, containing the Old Guard, came on a furious gallop along this road, preceded by the cavalry, the plain in front of them was seen to be covered with clouds of smoke, amid which were heard incessant explosions of artillery. Oudinot and Victor were struggling nobly to preserve the road open, but pressed as they were by superior numbers, another hour would have found it closed and Napoleon been too late.

Ahead of all his troops, he dashed forward with his escort to where the firing was heaviest, and lo, he saw before him the whole French army in full retreat. Suddenly the standards of the cuirasseurs announcing that the Emperor had come, were seen, and then a shout went up like the cry of delirious joy. As these tired veterans swept onward, bearing their stern chieftain in their midst, *"Vive l'Empereur"* rolled from rank to rank, till it died away amid the ex-

Ulm

plosions of cannon on the distant plain. The retreat was at once stopped along the whole line, columns of attack were formed, and the advancing enemy checked at all points.

Napoleon, satisfied with having effected this, ordered a halt, that his over-worked troops might get a little rest. The poor fellows who, exhausted as they were, would have charged the enemy's batteries without a murmur, glad of a little respite, sunk to sleep on the ground where they stood.

The next day Napoleon drove the allies from their position with great slaughter, and though the Old Guard carried its eagles triumphantly as ever, it was too exhausted to make a vigorous pursuit, by which the Bavarians were saved from utter ruin.

Two days after, February 18th, the battle of Montereau was fought. From early in the morning till late in the afternoon, Victor, and afterward Gerard, strove gallantly to carry the heights of Surville; the latter again and again leading his men up to the very mouths of forty pieces of artillery. But the sacrifice and valor were alike in vain. At length as evening approached, Napoleon came up on a gallop with the artillery and cavalry of the Old Guard. Supported by its guns, the Guard with loud shouts and resolute step, pressed forward, and storming over those flaming heights, swept them as with a single blow, of artillery, infantry, and cavalry, which rolled together down in wild confusion upon the bridge.

Sixty pieces of artillery of the Old Guard were then placed where the enemy's batteries had been all day long vomiting fire on the French columns of attack, and concentrated their close and deadly volleys upon the masses crowding frantically over the bridge. In his eagerness, Napoleon took charge of a cannon, pointing it himself. The cannoneers of the Old Guard, covered with powder and smoke, gazed with wonder on their Emperor discharging the duties of a common gunner, and as the shot of the enemy whistled around them, they besought him to retire from the danger. They cared not for themselves, they were accustomed to the crash of cannon balls, but they were filled with alarm to see the messengers of death filling the air around their beloved Emperor. But he replied gaily, as the light of early days flashed over his stern features, "Courage, my friends, the bullet which is to kill me is not yet cast."

The Horse Grenadiers Forcing the Defile

The allied army, shattered and bleeding, fled over the Seine, and joy and hope filled the bosom of Napoleon.

But while these extraordinary successes were dispelling the gloom that overhung the prospects of the Emperor, a new cloud was gathering on another portion of the French frontier. Bernadotte, whose fortunes Napoleon had made, and who, but for him, would never have been king of Sweden, whose crown the latter at any time could have crushed like a shell in his hand;—this weak-minded, selfish, ungrateful Gascon taking it into his conceited head that he might become Emperor of France, had entered his native country by way of Cologne, and with a powerful army was moving towards Paris.

Notwithstanding all this, the allied sovereigns were filled with terror and dismay at the rapid and terrible blows Napoleon had inflicted on them, and were anxious to come to terms with him before greater disasters should overtake them. With nearly two hundred thousand men, they had been scourged and humbled by seventy thousand; Blucher had lost twenty thousand, while Napoleon was weakened by not more than four thousand men. The army under Schwartzenberg too, within a few days had lost twelve thousand—in all nearly half as many men as the French Emperor had at any time brought into the field. The lion was awake again, and with his Old Guard was storming over their batteries and treading down their veteran troops as he had done at Jena, Austerlitz, and Friedland. They were alarmed, for they began to hear again his cannon thundering on the gates of their capitals. A treaty was proposed, but among other hard conditions which it contained, it required Napoleon to abandon all his conquests and restore France to the limits of the monarchy under Louis XIV. To the former part of the conditions he would consent, but to the latter, never. At Frankfort they had offered to let the Rhine form the boundary of France, and this he was now willingness to grant, great as the sacrifice was.

Many have blamed him for not accepting these terms, and reposing himself, till with recruited strength and means he might again take the field. This was the course Austria and Prussia had repeatedly pursued. When his armies were in their capitals, those monarchs would submit to any terms, inwardly resolved to violate the most sacred treaties the moment an opportunity occurred in which there was a prospect of success. Though allies with him in the invasion of Russia, they both turned against him when the disastrous retreat from Moscow had weakened his power. But Napoleon was as much above these sovereigns in magnanimity as he was in genius.

He would consent to nothing but a solid peace and one honorable to himself and the French people, and when urged by his minister, Maret, to yield to necessity, he made no reply, but taking up a volume of Montesquieu, read aloud, "I know nothing more magnanimous than the resolution which a monarch took who has reigned in our times (Louis XIV.) to bury himself under the ruins of his throne rather than accept conditions unworthy of a king. He had a mind too lofty to descend lower than his fortunes had sunk him, he knew well that courage may

179

strengthen a crown, but infamy never." Sustained by such a lofty resolution, he turned, sombre and stern and with an undaunted heart, on his foes.

It was unfortunate for him that he did not carry out his original plan of bringing Eugene from Italy to his aid. After his repulse at Rothiere, he sent a despatch to him to hasten across the Alps and threaten the allies in rear. This would have brought 40,000 fresh troops into the field, and at a dangerous point to the enemy. But his great successes gave him courage, and he countermanded the order. In fact he did not consider himself in so much peril as others did, for he had not lost a single battle, if we except the repulse at the outset, at Rothiere. He had met with but one repulse, while he and his Guard had swept every field on which they had struggled.

Having driven back the allies under Schwartzenberg, Napoleon again turned his attention to Blucher, who having recovered from the severe chastisement he had received, was marching rapidly on Paris. He had reached Meaux, only three days' march from the city, and the thunder of his cannon had been heard there, striking terror into the hearts of its inhabitants.

But this iron-willed Prussian, while exulting in the near prospect of beholding the French capital, was arrested with the stunning news that Napoleon with his Old Guard, was thundering in his rear. He immediately retreated in great haste toward Soissons, around which Bernadotte's army lay, in the hope to effect a junction with it and offer his pursuer battle. Soissons was deemed impregnable and was in possession of the French. Napoleon had sent to General Moreau, the commander, to defend it with his brave Poles, the remnant of Poniatowski's corps, to the "last drop of their blood." Instead of obeying this peremptory order, the cowardly or traitorous commander gave up the place without striking a blow, and that too just as Blucher was approaching it with his tattered, ragged, and exhausted army, feeling that he was marching on certain destruction. But for this shameful rendition, the army of Silesia would have been annihilated, and the whole aspect of the campaign changed.

Napoleon was thrown into a transport of rage at this unexpected overthrow of his sagacious combination, exclaiming, "the name of Moreau always brings misfortune." The weakness or crime of one commander, had sufficed to render all his skilful plans and wearisome marches fruitless. While he was expecting to deal a death-blow to the army of Silesia, and then turn back as before, and punish the tardy army, under Schwartzenberg, he saw the former join his troops to those of Bernadotte, swelling their forces to over a hundred thousand men, while he had not half that number under his command. It was enough to break the heart of a strong man to see genius and effort thus rendered useless, and such splendid combinations overthrown by the fault of one officer.

It seemed as if Fate was determined to drive this great soul to madness. Napoleon, however, with his exhausted army, moved forward and attacked the enemy in their almost impregnable position at Craonne. Prodigies of valor were performed in this bloody attack. Drouot in the midst of his guns, the Old Guard staggering under the fire of sixty cannon, wearied columns plunging with loud cheers on positions that looked unassailable, unbounded devotion of officers and men, combined to make it one of the most remarkable days of Napoleon's life. Still it was the Old Guard that wrought the miracles that paralyzed the enemy, and finally forced it to retire. In writing to Joseph, Napoleon said, "The Old Guard alone stood firm—the rest melted like snow." Alas, the Old Guard had also melted away, but only under the tremendous fire of the enemy's batteries, and on the spot where they stood.

Napoleon now saw that from the perils which environed him, nothing short of a miracle could deliver him, and while traversing this bloody battle-field in gloom, said, "I see clearly that this war is an abyss, but I will be the last to bury myself in it. If we must wear the fetters it is not I who will stretch out my hands to receive them."

Firm and calm he still stood at bay—nay, pushed boldly on the enemy. Following up the retreating armies of Blucher and Bernadotte to Laon, he resolved to give battle, though the enemy occupied an exceedingly strong position with a force more than double his own. It was a desperate resolution, but nothing short of desperate means could save him.

Having taken up his position in front of the place, he however waited the arrival of Marmont to whom he had sent despatches to join him, before venturing an attack. This marshal who, with great generalship, was always committing egregious blunders, was fast coming up, and on the 9th bivouacked within a few miles of Napoleon. The next day he would have effected a junction. Yet notwithstanding he was in the neighborhood of the enemy, with whom he had been engaged during the day, he allowed himself to be surprised at night, and utterly annihilated.

This unexpected disaster compelled Napoleon to retreat. It was with gloomy forebodings that after such prodigious efforts he took up his retrograde march without having struck a decisive blow.

Before he left Laon, however, he made the enemy feel the weight of his terrible Guard, which so daunted them that no pursuit was attempted.

Overmatched and exhausted as Napoleon now was, he still looked resolutely on the circle of fire that was steadily growing narrower around him. His great heart beat as firmly as in the hour of victory, and the depth of his anguish could be seen only by the increased sternness and gravity of his aspect. He seemed to be gazing gloomily into the future, and as he stood amid his unconquerable Guard, now no longer in complete uniform with burnished arms, but ragged and wan, besmeared with smoke and powder, he seemed the embodiment of thought surrounded by the shattered instruments of power. Those scarred veterans who had so often sent up the shout of victory at his presence, gazed on him with greater awe than ever. In the long and silent moods that came over him, they saw the terrible future before them. They were not accustomed to such constant fits of abstraction, and they jocularly called him "Father Thoughtful." Still their secret convictions belied their outward gaiety, for although they felt strong in their resolution and valor, they could not but see that the struggle was growing hopeless. To die for their Emperor was an easy task, but would that save him! Forgetting themselves, they thought only of him, as he, forgetting himself, thought only of France.

But though wearied and overtasked, his was a will that nothing could break—a heart that no danger or calamity could crush, and while Blucher was resting idle at Laon, he fell suddenly on Rheims, occupied by St. Priest with 14,000 men, and took it, relieving the army of a third of its number, together with its infamous commander. Here he had a last review of his Old Guard, and a sad spectacle those scarred veterans presented. For nearly two months they had marched over the most impassable roads, fought two armies each superior to their own, submitted to unparalleled fatigue without a murmur; and now haggard and wan, their uniform in tatters, their horses mere skeletons, their guns battered and black, all showing what privations and toil and incessant conflicts they had endured, they looked the mere wreck of their former selves. Still their appearance was nothing compared to that of the broken down young conscripts and other portions of the army. As Napoleon saw these last defile past him, a frown darkened his features, for "coming events were casting their shadows before," but when his glance fell on the eagles of the Old Guard, and he beheld their firm set ranks move by, a smile of triumph relaxed his stern expression, for he felt that he might not despair so long as that iron band closed around him.

No sooner was Schwartzenberg apprised of Napoleon's departure to arrest Blucher, than he advanced against the slight curtain of troops under Oudinot and Macdonald, left to dispute his advance to Paris. The French marshals were of course driven back, although obstinately contesting every inch of ground as they retired.

The serious aspect of affairs in this quarter hurried Napoleon back as before, but not victorious as then over Blucher.

His junction with Oudinot filled the allies with alarm, and Schwartzenberg hastily concentrated his forces, fearing one of those sudden and desperate blows the Emperor was accustomed to give with his Old Guard. The latter endeavored to manœuvre on the flank and rear of the enemy, but their rapid concentration prevented him, so that he was compelled to attack a force double his own, and the battle of Arcis-sar-Aube was fought.

On the first day Napoleon was in the midst of the Guard, who stood firm as a rock under one of the most terrific cannonades to which they had ever been exposed. Nearly every one of his staff was killed or wounded by his side. A bomb fell in front of one of the battalions of conscripts, which caused a sudden confusion in their ranks. Napoleon, conscious of his imminent peril unless his troops stood firm, spurred fiercely up to the shell and made his horse smell it. It burst, overthrowing both him and his steed. With the same impassible face, whose serenity no power on earth seemed able to disturb, he arose from his mutilated steed and calmly mounting another, stood with gloom on his brow, but grand and resolute as ever, in the vortex of the battle. Again and again he spurred at the head of his Guard on the most deadly batteries, and though all around him were struck, he seemed to bear a charmed life.

At ten at night the batteries ceased playing, and the two armies sunk to rest on the field they had piled with the dead.

The next day Napoleon seeing that it was useless to contend in such a position against an army so vastly superior to his own, commenced a retreat, which he effected in perfect order, though a hundred cannon were playing upon his retiring columns. The loss was nearly equal in this bloody engagement, and neither could claim the victory, but nothing now could arrest the double movement of the allies on Paris. Napoleon then saw the mistake he had made in not having relinquished his hold on Holland, Italy, and Spain, and brought up the veteran armies that were there struggling to retain his possessions. Still he did not despair, and hoped to divert the allies from their onward movement by marching back towards the Rhine, and falling on their communications. To his surprise, however, they let him go, and moved en masse upon Paris. When he at last discovered their determination, he wheeled about, and taking with him the Old Guard, strained every nerve to reach the city before its downfall. Previous to starting, however, he delivered another of his terrible blows on the force left to watch his movements.

The devoted Guard which had borne the weight of this campaign, which was called "Campaign of the Imperial Guard," and had made unparalleled marches and endured privations that would have broken the spirit and strength of any other soldiers in Europe, were now called upon to put forth still greater efforts. When Napoleon announced to them that the enemy was marching on Paris, and they must hasten to its relief, they answered him with a shout, and soon those brave men were seen moving like winged troops over the country. Although in the most frightful condition, having been without bread for the last six days, and for the most part barefoot, suffering grievously for the mere necessaries of life, they cheerfully traversed the miry roads in the midst of pelting storms, sternly crowding after their agitated, but still indomitable chief. A little after midnight of the 30th, they arrived at Troyes, having marched twenty-four hours without rest, making the astonishing distance of forty miles. But no troops could long stand such a strain, and Napoleon was compelled to leave them behind to rest a short time; and proceeded alone without any escort towards Paris. His agitation, wild ride, and distress and anger when he heard of the capitulation of the city, are well known. The thunderbolt had fallen.

But dark as the prospect now grew around him, he did not yield to despair. He had entered the capitals of every sovereign whose troops now swarmed through Paris. In their kingly palaces he had dictated terms to them and treated them like kings still, and they must reciprocate this treatment. But to his surprise those monarchs, who had not hesitated to make treaties with him up to the last moment, no sooner found themselves in possession of Paris, than they refused to recognise him as a legitimate sovereign. Ah, how deeply he must have regretted then the leniency he had shown them in former years, and bitterly remembered the hour when, with a single blow, he could have dismembered faithless Austria, but forbore.

Still his case was not hopeless—he had bivouacked amid the ashes of Moscow, but the Russian army did not die. He had bombarded Vienna, but the king remained; he had marched into Berlin, but the Prussian columns were not extinct. True, Paris had fallen and he looked round on a vast ruin; but the monarchs who spurned him now had looked upon as great a ruin wrought by his hands, and with less genius and resources than he possessed, had risen again, and he would show them the lion was not yet dead. He had not been beaten in a single battle—only once, and that in the first engagement at Rothiere, had he been even repulsed. With vastly inferior forces he had been victorious in every engagement.

Through constant defeats the enemy had entered his capital. He had been accustomed to march over routed armies into their capitals, but over him and that Old Guard they could not with their gathered millions go. They had succeeded because with his few troops he could not block every passage leading from the extended frontiers of France to its heart. With one army he could not spread himself the whole breadth of his empire and arrest the march of three armies. Against either one he was always successful, and but for accidents no man could anticipate, instead of beating these separately, he would have annihilated them in succession. But he had failed, and now he stood amid perils that might well daunt the stoutest heart. Still there was room for hope. Suchet had 20,000 veterans in Spain. Soult, who had retreated into France, had over 30,000. Marmont and Mortier, who had retired from Paris on its capture, had also a large army. Augereau was at the head of another, Prince Eugene of another, while his own forces numbered 60,000, among which, with spirits unbroken, was the steadfast Old Guard.

Besides all these, Davoust still held Hamburg, and Carnot Bergen op Zoom, which places, together with Magdebourg, Wesel, Mayence, Barcelona, Antwerp, Mantua, and Alexandria, contained over 90,000 men and twelve thousand cannon all at his disposal. One of the last shouts in the battle around Paris, was *"Vive l' Empereur,"* from some of the Old Guard who had fought like lions under Curial. His marshals—veterans tried in a hundred battles—also remained to him. Davoust, Suchet, Soult, Victor, Marmont, Mortier, Massena, Eugene, and Ney—hosts in themselves, were left. Not an army had been dissipated, and he could look around on a force vast enough, with him and his marshals at its head, to cope with Europe in arms against him.

At all events he would strike for his empire, so long as a blow could be given. Filled with this determination, he, at Fontainbleau, whither he had retired, immediately began to put his Guard in a proper condition for active service. Having made several changes among the commanding officers, he reviewed it. The infantry were ranged along two sides; fifteen deep, and after he had gone through their ranks, he called around him the older officers and soldiers of each company, and forming them in a circle, said:

"Soldiers, the enemy has stolen three marches on us, and entered Paris. We must drive them out of it. The unworthy French emigrants whom we have pardoned, have assumed the white cockade and jointed the enemy. The poltroons—they shall receive the reward of this new attempt. Let us swear to conquer or die, to make this tri-colored cockade respected, which, for twenty years, has always been found in the path of glory and honor."

With one voice they cried, "Yes, yes, we swear it, *Vive l'Empereur.*"

The infantry then defiled rapidly by and gave place to the cavalry which shook their sabres as they passed, crying, *"Vive l'Empereur."* This unconquerable corps had derived from its intrepid leader the indomitable will and heroic bearing in the midst of adversity. Though just relieved from unparalleled efforts and sufferings, worn down by fatigue, and needing repose, they were ready at his command to encounter still greater hardships and undergo still heavier privations. Over many a doubtful battle-field, through the snow and frosts of Russia, past flaming batteries, with their brave arms around him, they had carried him all steadily forward, and were ready again to enfold him in their solid squares, and bid defiance to the world in arms. Rising in moral grandeur above the most disheartening circumstances, above every selfish gratification and fear of peril or death, they stood there by their wrecked Emperor, the same "column of granite" to which again and again he had riveted his fortunes and his empire in safety.

Immediately after the review, the Guard took up their march for Essonnes, where Marmont lay with his army. They reached it late at night and encamped outside.

But when Marmont discovered that Napoleon, instead of bending to the storm was determined to breast it boldly, and again take the field, he opened secret negotiations with the allies, the result of which was, he, with his army, were to abandon the important position of Essonnes and join them. He accordingly at four o'clock in the morning of the 5th of April, having previously ordered that profound silence should be maintained in the ranks, took up his line of march.

This early departure and silent march was taken to deceive the troops, who supposed they were about to be led against the enemy. They did not discover their error till they saw the Bavarian army marching by their side, ready to arrest any movement which might be made against their commander. The Polish cavalry, however, no sooner saw how they had been betrayed, than they struck their spurs into their horses and bursting away, came in a fierce gallop to Fontainbleau, and reported the treason. When Napoleon heard it, he exclaimed:

"Who could have believed Marmont capable of such an act, a man with whom I have divided my bread, whom I drew from obscurity, whose fortune and reputation I made. The lot of sovereigns is to make ingrates. Ah, surely his troops did not know whither he was leading them, and yet he has always before this given me the most lively proofs of attachment."

Soon after, Ney began to vacillate—declaring it was useless to prosecute the war. The young generals were eager to march against the enemy, but the marshals and older officers were tired of the protracted conflict. Besides, the defection of Marmont had thrown a gloom over the whole army. His example was contagious, and a sudden revulsion of feeling and enthusiasm followed, and Napoleon saw that his veteran generals could not be relied upon. The allies took advantage of this state of things and immediately rose in their demands. At first they had stipulated that Napoleon should abdicate in favor of his son—now they required him to abdicate unconditionally. The senate taking courage, dethroned him. When this decision was brought him, he gave way to a torrent of indignation, and refused in the most peremptory manner to sign his abdication. With light flashing from his eyes, and his iron will written on every feature of his pale countenance, he declared he would put himself again at the head of his armies, and fall on the field of battle, rather than submit to such humiliation; and it was not till his marshals gave him to understand that they would not go with him, that he consented to yield.

In his formal abdication, which followed, he said:

"The powerful allies having proclaimed that the Emperor Napoleon is the only obstacle in the way of the peace of Europe, The Emperor Napoleon, faithful to his oath, declares that he renounces for himself and his heirs, the thrones of France and Italy, since it is not merely any personal sacrifice, but that of his life he would make for the interests of France." He then conversed with the generals of his Guard, saying, "Now that all is ended, and I can no longer remain here, your interest is with the Bourbon family. It will rally all parties. The king, they say, has judgment and discretion. He will not wish, I think, to attach his name to a bad reign. If he is wise, in occupying my bed at the Tuilleries, he will only change the drapery. If his family are wise, you will be happy, but he must treat the army well, and not attempt to bring back the past, otherwise, his reign will be short."

Thus he went on uttering truths that a Bourbon could never understand, till driven from his throne. His abdication was followed by the most shameful desertion, which broke his spirit more than all the disasters which for the last two years had accumulated upon him, or the loss of his throne.

"After it," says Caulincourt, his grand equery, "every hour was marked by fresh voids in the Emperor's household. The universal object was how to get first to Paris. All persons in office quitted their places without leave, or even asking permission; one after another they all slipped away, totally forgetting him to whom they owed everything, but who no longer had anything to give. The universal complaint was, that he so long delayed the formal announcement of his abdication. 'It was high time,' every one said, 'for all this to come to an end; it is absolute childishness to remain any longer in the anti-chambers of Fontainbleau when favors are showering down at Paris,' and with that they all set out for the capitol. Such was their anxiety to hear of his abdication, that they pursued misfortune even into its last asylum; and every time the door of the cabinet opened, a crowd of heads was seen peeping in to gain the first hint of the much longed-for news."

His household was deserted of men of distinction, with the exception of Maret and Caulincourt. Even his valet Constant, who had served him fourteen years, stole a hundred thousand francs and ran away, and the Mameluke Roustan, with him. The defection reached the army. Berthier left him without even a formal adieu. When Napoleon heard of his departure, he said scornfully:

"He was born a courtier; you will see my vice-constable mendicating employment from the Bourbons. I feel mortified that men whom I have raised so high in the eyes of Europe should sink so low. What have they made of that halo of glory through which they have hitherto been seen by the stranger. What must the sovereigns think of such a termination to those who have illustrated my reign."

The old generals whom he had covered with glory hastened to offer their swords to their new master, and in the struggle on every side for place and preferment, Napoleon was abandoned. This was an unexpected blow, and it broke him down. That will of iron and soul of indomitable courage that no misfortune or danger could shake, and he who, when alone, could bend his haughty brow on the sovereigns of Europe, greater in his isolation than they in their triumphs, sunk under the desertion of his followers. It was the only time in his life that he ever exhibited weakness, and he resolved to take his own life.

Those around him observed a strangeness of demeanor, as if the present was forgotten, and something remote and mysterious absorbed his thoughts. He spoke of the heroes of antiquity who would not survive their misfortunes, and on the night of the 12th, on taking leave of Caulincourt, he said with a look of settled melancholy:

"My resolution is taken; we must end, I feel it."

A few hours after, Caulincourt was awakened by Napoleon's valet, who rushing in, said that the Emperor was in convulsions and dying. As he reached the apartment, he saw Maret and Bertrand standing over the bed, from which arose stifled groans wrung by agony from the breast of the royal sufferer. Soon after Ivan, his surgeon, ran in greatly terrified; for he had seen Napoleon shortly after retiring, rise and pour some liquid from a vial and drink it. This liquid he had just discovered to be a subtle poison he himself mixed for the Emperor when in Russia, to be taken in the last emergency, if captured by the Cossacks. Caulincourt leaned over him and took his hand and found it already cold. The Emperor opened his eyes and said in a feeble voice:

"Caulincourt, I am about to die. I recommend to you my wife and son—defend my memory. I could no longer endure life. The desertion of my old companions in arms had broken my heart."

The bolt had come from his brave "companions in arms" with whom he had toiled over so many battle-fields, shared so many hardships, and triumphed together in so many victories, and whose renown was a part of his own.

The dose, however, probably from being kept so long proved too weak, and after the most excruciating agony for two hours, he was relieved by violent vomiting. The spasms gradually became less severe, and at length he fell asleep. On awaking he said, "Ivan, the dose was not strong enough—God did not will it ;" and from that moment his wonted serenity returned, and he began to make preparations for his departure.

But amid this general abandonment, there was an exhibition of attachment and fidelity which more than compensated for all the disgrace in which the mighty drama was closing, and threw a halo of glory around the closing scene, worthy of Napoleon and his career. The Old Guard to a man stood firm. Not one in that vast body would leave him. Rock-fast in its affection, as in its courage, it was above the contagion of selfish example as it had ever been above that of fear. Those stern veterans saw with scorn the base abandonment of their chief, and closed around him more devotedly than ever. True, he had nothing more to give them. A banished and powerless man, they could gain nothing by adhering to his fallen fortunes but disgrace and suspicion. It mattered not; in their frozen bivouacks, on the field of carnage, in the midst of famine, and in the triumph of victory, they had enfolded him in their protecting squares, and they would not desert him now. Grand like their chief, they scorned to stoop to meanness for self-preservation. They all, with one accord, demanded permission to accompany him in his exile. This the allies would not grant; only four hundred were permitted to go as a bodyguard, while fifteen hundred might escort him to the seaside, where he was to embark.

The 20th of April was fixed for his departure, and after one more struggle, the great drama would close—he was yet to bid farewell to his faithful Guard, his companions by night and day for so many years, and through so many trying scenes. These veterans, with tears in their eyes, stood in the court of Chevalblanc, drawn up in two ranks, waiting to take farewell forever of their beloved commander. At noon he descended the stairs of the palace, and walking through the throng of carriages waiting at the door, stepped into the midst of the Old Guard, which immediately closed in a circle around him. Casting his eye over the familiar ranks, he said, in a calm but subdued voice:

"Officers and soldiers of my Guard, I bid you adieu. For twenty years I have led you in the path of victory—for twenty years you have served me with honor and fidelity—receive my thanks. My aim has always been the happiness and glory of France. To-day circumstances are changed. When all Europe is armed against me, when all the princes and powers have leagued together, when a great portion of my empire is seized, and a part of France. . . ." He paused a moment at these words, and then in an altered voice continued, "When another order of things is established, I ought to yield.

"With you and the brave men who remained devoted to me, I could have resisted all the efforts of my enemies, but I should have kindled a civil war in our beautiful France—in the bosom of our beloved country.

"Do not abandon your unhappy country; submit to your chiefs, and continue to march in the road of honor where you have always been found. Grieve not over my lot, great remembrances remain with me. I shall occupy my time nobly in writing my history and yours.

"Officers and soldiers, I am content with you. I am not able to embrace you all, but I will embrace your general. Adieu, my children, adieu, my friends, preserve me in your memory. I shall be happy when I hear that you are so." Then turning to General Petit, he said, "Come, General."

Petit approached, and Napoleon pressed him to his overburdened breast. He then asked for the eagle that he might embrace that also. The standard-bearer inclined the eagle; Napoleon kissed it three times, every feature working with the intensity of his feelings.

"Ah, dear eagle," said he, and after a pause in which it seemed for a moment that his firmness would give way before the swelling tide of emotion that struggled for utterance, he added tenderly, "Adieu, my children, adieu my braves, surround me once again."

Those scarred veterans had never seen their chief so moved before, and as they stood and gazed in mournful silence on him whom they were to see no more, great tears rolled down their scarred visages, and their lion hearts were broken with grief. Napoleon threw one glance upon them and their eagle, then tore himself away, and flinging himself into a carriage, drove off toward the place where he was to embark.

The silence that reigned in the ranks after his disappearance, the mournful aspects of the men, the utter loneliness which every one felt, showed what a place Napoleon held in their affections. It was the love the brave always bear the brave who have combated by their sides. The scene was worthy of the actors in it, and Napoleon could not have had a more glorious termination to his great career.

The world never witnessed any thing more indomitable than Napoleon and that Old Guard; the earth never shook under anything more terrible than their tread, and the eye of man never gazed on more terrific scenes than they had moved amid unappalled, yet here at the last they were melted to tears. It was a scene to touch the hardest heart, and the allied officers who had been sent to accompany Napoleon at his departure, could not repress their emotion in witnessing it. A hundred fields of fame seemed to look down on them there—great remembrances clustered around them. From the dazzling splendor of the pyramids—from the Alps, the Pyrenees, from Italy, from the Rhine, the Danube, and the Niemen, the eye turned to that last adieu, scarcely convinced that that was the end of it all.

Fontainbleau was deserted, and the Old Guard took up its march for Paris. In the imposing pageants the allied sovereigns kept up in the capital, it too was compelled to make a part, and was seen side by side with the Russian, Prussian, and Austrian Guards. Yet even here the veterans bore the same undaunted aspect, and looked more like conquerors than conquered. Their masters, but not their victors, were about them. They might assume the relation of conquerors, but never on the field of battle had they earned the right to do so. In the very last struggle which ended in the overthrow of the empire, not once had they been beaten, while before their charge the firm-est ranks of their foes had been shivered into fragments. The very last time they had moved with levelled bayonets on the enemy, they had trampled them under foot, and why should they feel like vanquished men!

It was this very consciousness of never having been beaten, and the firm belief they could not be, that made the position they were compelled to occupy so hateful, and gave them a sternness of expression and haughtiness of bearing that attracted every beholder. With the same steady step that had made Europe tremble, they defiled before their new masters, while their sullen aspects and scornful looks gave rise to many dark suspicions and se-cret fears. Fields of slaughter rose one after another in dark succession as they passed, telling of deeds of valor undreamed of before.

So sullen was their humor, and so irritable did they be-come in their humiliating position, that they constantly sought quarrels with their enemies.

When Louis XVIII. entered Paris, the grenadiers of the Guard maintained a gloomy silence, none but the dragoons and guards of honor could be prevailed upon to cry *"Vive le Roi."* These old veterans refused to obey their officers in this respect, and when the review was past, they shouted, *"Vive l'Empereur."*

Usually distinguished for their peaceable deportment, the soldiers now became intractable, and duels with the troops of the allied army were of daily occurrence.

One day the Austrian grenadiers appeared with green sprigs in their caps. This, the Old Guard took as a sign of triumph, and immediately insulted them, daring them to battle. Such was its rage at their presuming to wear pub-licly a badge of triumph when they had been beaten on every field of Europe, that Schwartzenberg had to write the French minister of war on the subject, and caused to be put in the Paris journals an article stating that these "green branches were not designed as a mark of triumph, but a simple rallying sign, prescribed from time immemorial by military rules both in peace and war."

Savage and morose, the Old Guard trod the streets of Paris on review in silence, but when in their barracks their indignation found open vent, and their "Vive l' Empereur" was often heard.

So grievously did they take the altered state of things.

CHAPTER 12

1815: The Old Guard Under the Restoration

The aspect of affairs did not improve much after the allied troops left Paris. The Old Guard on the one hand was an object of suspicion and fear—on the other it scorned the new system of things. As for Marmont, its contempt for him was open and undisguised. For the traitor who had brought about their humiliation they had nothing but maledictions. Louis XVIII. would gladly have disbanded the corps but he dared not.

There was no bond of sympathy between it and a Bourbon, and to serve him after being the prop and pride of Napoleon was as mortifying as to be taunted by the stranger. In fact there was something twice as regal about the bearing and aspect of the Guard, as there was in the king himself. Still Louis commenced by flattering and caressing it. He eulogized it and was prodigal of promises. He told the marshals that he wished to look upon the Guard as his stay and defence, and went so far as to toast it at a public dinner. But he could make no advance in its affections—proud of its old renown, sore from recent humiliations, nothing seemed able to satisfy it. To complete and make permanent the breach, the king ordered the tri-color to be thrown aside. It was decreed that the mere wearing of it should be considered open rebellion. This was accusing those who composed the Old Guard of crime, when under these colors they were shedding their blood on the soil of France to keep it from being defiled by the foot of the stranger. But it was to them a cherished symbol reminding them of their deeds of renown. In many a deadly encounter they had clung to the tri-colored standard with a tenacity nothing could shake. They had pressed after it through fire and blood, and over ranks of living men.

From the vortex of the battle, whither they had carried it, they had seen it emerge riddled with balls and singed with flame, but still triumphantly streaming in the wind. They had sworn to defend it, and die rather than surrender it, and no mortal power had ever been able to wrench it from their grasp. They had seen it wave by the pyramids and droop along the glaciers of the Alps. Over countless fortresses and cities they had lifted it in triumph. They had watched it fluttering amid the flames of Moscow, and closed firmly around it when beat upon by the storms of a Russian winter. It had watched with them around their frozen bivouacs, and had become endeared to them by a thousand struggles to preserve it untarnished; they had baptized it in their own blood, and it had been their companion through years of toil and suffering, and now to surrender it at the command of a Bourbon—to let it drop ignobly from their hands when through such perils and death struggles, they had held it with a firm grasp, filled them with indignation and grief.

That tri-color flag had made the tour of Europe with them, and was at once the symbol of their glory and the history of their needs. Enraged at the command to exchange it for the white flag, many of the regiments burned their colors rather than part with them, and preserved the ashes as a sacred relic. Most of the soldiers wore the tri-colored cockade underneath the white one, and the eagles were hidden away to preserve them. They were changed into "the royal corps of France," but they had some mementoes left to show they were still the Old Guard of Napoleon.

But the old order of things was to be re-established, and not only were the national colors changed but the Guard itself underwent modifications so as to efface, as much as possible, the remembrance of the deeds that had immortalized it. Its officers were left in penury and want, and nobles of the old regime filled all places of honor and emolument.

This ridiculous conduct on the part of the king, completed the alienation of the Guard, and its bearing became so fierce and threatening that it was sent from Paris.

But the injustice and oppression under which it suffered did not produce such open indignation as the taunts and insults the officers and their wives received—the former from courtiers and the latter from even courtesans, who were in the favor of Louis, and the contemptible attacks in the newspapers on Napoleon. These latter called him a fool—declared that he had become an object of pity and derision, that all his troops had abandoned him gladly and returned to France to range themselves under the untarnished flag of the Bourbons. These things were discussed by officers and men in their quarters, and deep though smothered threats of vengeance uttered.

Soon after, a conspiracy was set on foot to bring back Napoleon. The officers of the Old Guard were deeply implicated in it, and occasional intimations reached the soldiers filling them with joy, for they burned to see their emperor once more in their midst. They were heard to say, "he will reappear to chase away with a look these emigrants who have insulted our ancient glory.

The Island of Elba was erected by the allies into a sovereignty for Napoleon, of which he took possession, May 4th. He who had swayed an empire that reached from the Baltic to the Mediterranean, and at whose imperial voice nearly a million and a half of men stood up in order of battle, now had a kingdom eight miles long and two miles broad, and an army of four hundred men to protect it. It was one of those terrible reverses of fortune it seems strange the human mind can endure without the overthrow of reason.

To be hurled from the throne of such a vast empire and such heights of grandeur and power to the dominion of a little island, was a mockery more bitter to bear than death. Napoleon, however, met his fate with the dignity and serenity of a great mind. His first care on his arrival was his Old Guard. He organized it into six companies with a staff, and added a company of marines, and also a company of Polish lancers to which he gave the name of the "Squadron Napoleon."

He provided clean and comfortable barracks, and all the necessaries of life for this little army, and then turned his attention to his new kingdom. Instead of sitting down in sullen gloom or devoting himself solely to pleasure in order to prevent time from hanging heavy on his hands, he went to work with the same zeal and cheerfulness he did, when an empire was under his control. He developed the resources of the island, and gave a new impulse to industry and commerce. He ordered new mines to be opened, grounds drained, and everything done to advance the interests or ameliorate the condition of his subjects.

He rose early in the morning, and accompanied by Bertrand or Drouot, rode over different parts of the island to see how his little kingdom was getting on. After breakfast he reviewed his miniature army, as he was accustomed to review the

Old Guard in the court of the Tuileries. He would manœuvre these sometimes, for several hours. It seemed to amuse him and bring back those scenes of grandeur with which he had astonished the world. He devoted himself also to literature, and by his cheerfulness and urbanity, made all happy about him.

Sometimes he would go on foot to different points of the island, enter the stores and make purchases or leave orders, and terminate his tour at the barracks of the Guard, by which he was always received with loud acclamations.

But the old veterans, accustomed to a life of activity, and when in barracks to the variety and pleasure of a city, grew weary of this isolation, and together with the officers, pined for a different sphere of action. In order to drive away these feelings Napoleon obtained a company of comedians from Trieste and Naples, and set up a little theatre for their entertainment. The soldiers beheld again the Vaudevilles which had delighted them in Paris, and soon they were heard at all hours of the day humming some familiar song which these exhibitions recalled to mind.

Still the prospect of a life of idleness and exile was not very cheering, and Napoleon saw with regret the growing desire among officers and men to change their residence for one more congenial to their tastes. One day on entering the barracks of his Guard, while they were preparing dinner, he said pleasantly to a group standing near him, "Well, my grumblers, is the soup good to-day?"

"Yes, my Emperor," said one of the old scarred veterans, "but it would be better if ————"

"If what," replied Napoleon, "is not the meat good, and the vegetables, are they tough?" "On the contrary," responded the grenadier, "the meat and vegetables are excellent, but one thing is wanting which it is not in your power to give."

"What's that, speak, let us see?" demanded Napoleon impatiently.

"Water of the Seine to boil them in," said the veteran coolly, and without changing a muscle of his countenance.

Napoleon smiled bitterly at the hit, exclaiming, as he walked away, "Bah! bah! one can eat a partridge very well without an orange. You are too much of a gourmet."

At another time as he was walking at evening, as he was accustomed to do, backwards and forwards through the long avenues of sycamores that bordered the grounds of his palace toward the sea, he came suddenly upon an old grenadier sitting at the foot of a tree looking very melancholy.

"What are you doing here alone?" he demanded brusquely; "what are you thinking about?"

The soldier sprang to his feet with the military salute, and seeing a smile on the Emperor's face replied frankly, "I was thinking, my Emperor, of my country, and I said to myself, this is the close of the harvest time there."

"From what country are you?"

"From Antram, four leagues from Rennes, in Brittany."

"Brittany," exclaimed Napoleon, "is a very good country, a country of brave men, but a villainous heaven, it always rains there, while here the climate is sweet, the days are superb, and the sky resplendent. The isle of Elba is a much better place to live in than Brittany."

"My Emperor," replied the home-sick old soldier, "I am too honest to deceive you, but saving your majesty, I love the rain which falls at Antram better than the beautiful days of Elba, it is my idea, and I may say it without offending your majesty."

"But," continued Napoleon, "why don't you amuse yourself like your comrades? You have leisure, the wine is good, and you have the theatre to divert you; go to the theatre."

"That's true, my Emperor, but the pieces at the theatre do not equal those punchinellos of the boulevards of the Temple—that's something amusing."

"Ah, well," said Napoleon, as he walked away, "have patience; perhaps some day you will see again the boulevards of the Temple and its punchinellos." He repeated this conversation at evening and smiled at the simplicity and frankness of the old grenadier. The story soon got wind, and "I love better the panchinellos," was in every one's mouth. It had struck a responsive chord in the heart of each, and it was soon apparent how universal the grenadier's sentiment had become, for it gave them a way of expressing their feelings without offence.

Speaking of it one day, Drouot said to Napoleon, "We make poor Robinson Crusoes, and we do not resemble much Telemachus, in the isle of Calypso; for I presume if Minerva should appear among us in the shape of Mentor, she would not find it necessary to throw us into the sea in order to drive us from the island."

"Ah! that is it," said Napoleon, rubbing his hands, "if there now were a Calypso here, one would have to pull you by the ears to get you, like the son of Ulysses, back to Ithaca. The truth is, I have spoiled the whole of you. I have let you see too many countries and have accustomed you to such a moving existence, that you are not able to enjoy a philosophic repose." Then turning to some officers who stood by, he said, "Allons, Messieurs, if you are wise, perhaps I will let you make some time a tour in France." But perceiving he had said too much, he pressed his lips together, and forcing a pinch of snuff violently up his nose, abruptly changed the conversation.

Return of Napoleon and His Guard to France

On the 26th of February, 1815, Col. Laborde received orders from Drouot to let all the laborers in the gardens of the officers continue their work till three o'clock—at four to give the troops soup, and immediately after assemble them. At five they were to embark in ships prepared for their reception. The Colonel enquired where they were going.

"I can tell you nothing," he replied, "execute the orders I have given you."

This being accomplished, Napoleon, after bidding his mother and sister Pauline adieu, went onboard the brig of war Inconstant, and with three hundred of his Guard, put to sea. The rest of the Guard and troops, in all some six or seven hundred men, followed in several transports. When fairly out to sea, Napoleon walked into the midst of his Guard, and said, "Soldiers and officers of my Guard, we are going to France." Loud shouts of "Vive l'Empereur," answered him, and all was enthusiasm and joy.

Only one vessel hailed them on the way, the captain of which asked if they had come from Elba. Being answered in the affirmative, he inquired how Napoleon was. The Emperor having ordered the Guard to lie flat on deck so as to prevent discovery, himself replied, "il se porte à merveille." The brig suspecting nothing passed along, and on the first of March, Napoleon reached the coast of France. Drouot immediately landed with the Old Guard and despatched a captain with a company of chasseurs to a garrison at Antibes to feel the pulse of the soldiers. The latter was taken prisoner with all his company, and two officers sent to demand their release shared the same fate.

That night Napoleon bivouacked in an olive field with his Old Guard around him. But at eleven o'clock he took up his march for Grasse, where he arrived at eleven in the morning. The soldiers were in a state of the highest enthusiasm. Napoleon had promoted every one of them, and now, as they saw him marching in their midst again, they thought of the glory of the past, and beheld new fields of fame in the future.

The triumphal march of Napoleon with that little band of less than a thousand men from Cannes to Paris is well known. Fortified towns and cities opened their gates to him; troops sent forward to capture him, shouted "Vive l' Empereur," as they caught sight again of the form of their old commander; officers and generals were swept away in the wild enthusiasm that increased as he advanced towards Paris, and borne along on the swelling heart of the nation, he entered his capital, and without firing a shot sat down on his recovered throne. The city was delirious with joy, and never in the height of his power did Napoleon receive such marks of unbounded devotion.

In his proclamation issued at Grenoble, calling on the soldiers to rally to his standard, who, he said, "had elevated him on their bucklers to the throne," he declared that "victory would march at the pas de charge, the eagle fly with the national colors from steeple to steeple till it lighted on the towers of Notre Dame." His prediction proved true. Victory had gone at the charge step, and the eagle flown from steeple to steeple in triumph.

The next day after his triumphal entrance into the city, the Old Guard arrived by post from Lyons. As the Emperor approached Paris, the news of the reception that waited him, made him precipitate his advance, and the Old Guard was left behind. But now as these few hundred veterans, whose worn shoes and tattered garments testified to their rapid and fatiguing march across France, came thundering into the city in carriages, long and deafening shouts rent the air. They had been the companions of their Emperor in his exile; the iron band on which he had relied in his daring descent on France; they seemed a part of him, and hence were objects of almost equal enthusiasm.

During the day, Napoleon had a grand review of all the troops in Paris. After it was over, he formed them into a square and addressed them. The acclamations that succeeded had scarcely died away, when a column of strange troops were seen advancing up the Place du Carrousel. As they approached with their standard in tatters, but carrying the eagles of the Old Guard, the army saw it was the sacred battalion that had accompanied Napoleon from Elba, and had just arrived by post from Lyons. As these veterans drew near, the drums throughout rolled forth a thundering salute, and banners waved, and swords shook in the air, and frantic hurrahs arose on every side.

Napoleon with a gesture of the hand having silenced the tumult, exclaimed, "Behold the battalion which accompanied me in my misfortune. They are all my friends, and they have been dear to my heart. Every time that I saw them they reminded me of the different regiments of the army, for among these six hundred braves there are men from all the regiments. They recalled to me the grand achievements, the memory of which is so dear, for they are all covered with honorable scars received in those memorable battles. In loving them, I love you all, soldiers of the French army. They bring back to you the eagles. In giving them to the Guard, I give them to the whole army. Treason and misfortune had covered them with a mournful veil, but they now reappear resplendent in their old glory. Swear to me that these eagles shall always be found where the welfare of the country calls them, and then those who would invade our soil will not be able to meet their glance." "We swear it, we swear it," was repeated in prolonged echoes on every side.

On the very day of his arrival Napoleon reorganized the Old Guard by a decree in which it was specified that no one should be admitted in it but "those who had served in the French army." Among the officers that were appointed to command it, Drouot took his old place, the brave Friant commanded the foot grenadiers, Morand the foot chasseurs, Guyot the mounted grenadiers, and Lefebvre Desnouettes the mounted chasseurs. These had been tried on many a field of fire and blood, and could be trusted. Still the Guard was formed in great haste, and though it had been augmented to 40,000, only a part of them possessed the character of the troops that formerly composed it. This was soon seen in the lax discipline that was maintained.

The allies knowing that every day given to Napoleon multiplied his resources, began immediately to pour vast armies towards the French borders. Not willing to let the French people choose their own ruler, they, without offering any terms of peace, deliberately resolved to deluge Europe in blood again, to keep a Bourbon on the throne.

The history of the "hundred days," in which Napoleon raised an army of nearly 400,000 men and took the field in the almost hopeless struggle against such immense forces as were pledged to his overthrow, is well known. In a letter to the allies, he begged them earnestly not to disturb the peace of Europe. After defending his course in ascending the throne of France on the ground that the Bourbons were not fitted for the French people, and stating how he had been borne on their hearts to the capital, he used the following noble language:

> The first wish of my heart is to repay so much affection by an honorable tranquillity. My sweetest hope is to render the reestablishment of the Imperial throne a guarantee for the peace of Europe. Enough of glory has illustrated in their turn the standards of all nations; the vicissitudes of fate have sufficiently often made great reverses follow the most glorious success. A nobler arena is now opened to sovereigns. I will be the first to descend into it. After having exhibited to the world the spectacle of great combating, it will now be sweeter to exhibit henceforth no other rivalry but that of the advantage of peace—no other strife but that of the felicity of nations.

To this appeal the allied sovereigns deigned not even a reply. This plebeian who had covered them with confusion, should not rule the people that loved him, so they struck hands together, Austria, Prussia, Russia, and agreed to furnish a hundred and eighty thousand men each, to carry on the war. Over seven hundred thousand men were to be banded against Napoleon. The contest, of course, was desperate, for France could not always keep at bay the whole of Europe in arms. And yet writers never tire of putting on Napoleon the crime of the carnage of Waterloo—a battle he did not wish to fight.

He was not prepared for hostilities, but was forced into them by those who after the field was heaped with the dead and Europe filled with mourning, turned round and pointed at him, exclaiming, what a monster! A monster for struggling with almost superhuman energy to prevent the invasion of his country by enemies whose only excuse was, they did not wish Napoleon to occupy the throne of France. Against Russia, Prussia, Austria, and England, does the blood from Waterloo cry out for vengeance. Nay, more, the slaughter that soon followed in the streets of Paris in the effort to get rid of this very sovereign they forced on France, lies at their doors. Already is Europe reaping the reward of her deeds, but the day of final reckoning has not yet come.

The old officers of the army and even the soldiers of the Guard looked upon the contest with dismay, but the younger officers and men, dreaming of Austerlitz, Friedland, and Wagram, were filled with enthusiasm. But though the old veterans looked grave and thoughtful, they determined to battle bravely for victory, and if it could not be won, to die on the field of honor.

On the 7th of June Napoleon set out for head-quarters, and a few days after, at the head of a hundred and fifty thousand men, boldly threw himself between Blucher and Wellington. He fell on the former at Ligny, and defeated him with the loss of fifteen thousand men. Drouot's artillery, with the columns of the Old Guard, moved against the centre of the Prussian army as of old, and pressing on over batteries and through clouds of cavalry, swept the field.

This admirable piece of strategy by which Napoleon separated the Prussian and English army, under ordinary circumstances would have secured him the campaign. Wellington had been completely out-generalled, and Napoleon never was more sure of victory than when he heard that his antagonist had retreated to Waterloo. There is no doubt there were traitors in his staff, for the despatch he sent Grouchy during the night, never reached him, while, in all probability it fell into the hands of Blucher. But, notwithstanding all this, had it not been for the heavy rain the night before rendering the ground too soft for artillery and cavalry to manœuvre, so that the attack was necessarily delayed, Napoleon would inevitably have beaten Wellington before Blucher could have arrived.

Charge of the Old Guard at Waterloo

Although I have this charge in another work yet being the last act in its history, the closing up of its long and brilliant career, I will venture here to repeat it, giving some additional details.

During the day the artillery of the Guard, under Drouot, maintained its old renown, and the Guard itself had frequently been used to restore the battle in various parts of the field, and always with success. The English were fast becoming exhausted, and in an hour more would doubtless have been forced into a disastrous retreat, but for the timely arrival of Blucher. But when they saw him with his 30,000 Prussians approaching, their courage revived, while Napoleon was filled with amazement. A beaten enemy was about to form a junction with the allies, while Grouchy, who had been sent to keep him in check, was nowhere to be seen. Alas, what great plans a single inefficient commander can overthrow.

In a moment Napoleon saw that he could not sustain the attack of so many fresh troops if once allowed to form a junction with the allied forces, and he determined to stake his fate on one bold cast and endeavor to pierce the allied centre with a grand charge of the Old Guard, and thus throw himself between the two armies. For this purpose the Imperial Guard was called up and divided into two immense columns, which were to meet in the British centre. Those under Reille no sooner entered the fire than it disappeared like mist. The other was placed under Ney, "the bravest of the brave," and the order to advance given. Napoleon accompanied them part way down the slope, and halting for a moment in a hollow, addressed them a few words. He told them the battle rested with them, and that he relied on their valor tried in so many fields. "Vive l' Empereur," answered him with a shout that was heard above the thunder of artillery.

The whole continental struggle exhibits no sublimer spectacle than this last effort of Napoleon to save his sinking empire. The greatest military energy and skill the world possessed had been tasked to the utmost during the day. Thrones were tottering on the turbulent field, and the shadows of fugitive kings flitted through the smoke of battle. Bonaparte's star trembled in the zenith—now blazing out in its ancient splendor, now suddenly paling before his anxious eye. At last he staked his empire on one bold throw. The intense anxiety with which he watched the advance of that column, and the terrible suspense he suffered when the smoke of battle wrapped it from sight, and the utter despair of his great heart when the curtain lifted over a fugitive army and the despairing shriek rung out, "The Guard recoils, the Guard recoils," make us for a moment forget all the carnage, in sympathy with his distress.

The Old Guard felt the pressure of the immense responsibility, and resolved not to prove unworthy of the great trust committed to its care. Nothing could be more imposing than its movement to the assault. It had never recoiled before a human foe, and the allied forces beheld with awe its firm and steady advance to the final charge. For a moment the batteries stopped playing, and the firing ceased along the British lines; as without the beating of a drum, or a bugle note to cheer their steady courage, they moved in dead silence over the field. Their tread was like the sound of muffled thunder, while the dazzling helmets of the cuirassiers flashed long streams of light behind the dark and terrible mass that swept in one strong wave along. The stern Drouot was there amid his guns, and on every brow was written the unalterable resolution to conquer or die.

The next moment the artillery opened, and the head of that gallant column seemed to sink into the earth. Rank after rank went down, yet they neither stopped nor faltered. Dissolving squadrons, and whole battalions disappearing one after another in the destructive fire, affected not their steady courage.

The ranks closed up as before, and each treading over his fallen comrade, pressed unflinchingly on. The horse which Ney rode, fell under him, and scarcely had he mounted another before it also sunk to the earth, and so another and another, till five in succession had been shot under him; then with his drawn sabre, he marched sternly at the head of his column. In vain did the artillery hurl its storm of fire and lead into that living mass. Up to the very muzzles they pressed, and driving the artillerymen from their pieces, pushed on through the English lines. But just as the victory seemed won, a file of soldiers who had lain flat on the ground behind a low ridge of earth, suddenly rose and poured a volley in their very faces. Another and another followed, till one broad sheet of flame rolled on their bosoms, and in such a fierce and unexpected flow that they staggered back before it.

Before the Guard had time to rally again and advance, a heavy column of infantry fell on its left flank in close and deadly volleys, causing it in its unsettled state to swerve to the right. At that instant a whole brigade of cavalry thundered on the right flank, and penetrated where cavalry had never gone before. That intrepid Guard could have borne up against the unexpected fire from soldiers they did not see, and would also have rolled back the infantry that had boldly charged its left flank, but the cavalry finished the disorder into which they had been momentarily thrown and broke the shaken ranks before they had time to reform, and the eagles of that hitherto invincible Guard were pushed backward down the slope.

It was then that the army seized with despair shrieked out, "The Guard recoils, the Guard recoils," and turned and fled in wild dismay. To see the Guard in confusion, was a sight they had never before beheld, and it froze every heart with terror. Still those veterans refused to fly; rallying from their disorder they formed into two immense squares of eight battalions and turned fiercely on the enemy, and nobly strove to stem the reversed tide of battle.

For a long time they stood and let the cannon balls plough through their ranks, disdaining to turn their backs to the foe. Michel, at the head of those brave battalions, fought like a lion. To every command of the enemy to surrender, he replied, "The Guard dies, it never surrenders," and with his last breath bequeathing this glorious motto

WATERLOO

to the Guard, he fell a witness to its truth. Death traversed those eight battalions with such a rapid footstep, that they soon dwindled to two, which turned in hopeless daring on the overwhelming numbers that pressed their retiring footsteps. Last of all but a single battalion, the debris of the "column of granite" at Marengo, was left. Into this Napoleon flung himself.

Cambronne, its brave commander, saw with terror the Emperor in its frail keeping. He was not struggling for victory, he was intent only on showing how the Guard should die. Approaching the Emperor, he cried out, "Retire, do you not see that death has no need of you?" and closing mournfully yet sternly round their expiring eagles, those brave hearts bade Napoleon an eternal adieu, and flinging themselves on the enemy, were soon piled with the dead at their feet.

Many of the officers were seen to destroy themselves rather than survive defeat. Thus, greater in its only defeat than any other corps of men in gaining a victory, the Old Guard passed from the stage, and the curtain dropped upon its strange career. It had fought its last battle.

No one can contemplate this termination of its history without the profoundest emotion. The greatness of its deeds and the grandeur of its character, endear it to all who love heroic action and noble achievements; and as one runs back in imagination, over its terrible campaigns, it is with the deepest sorrow he is compelled to bid it farewell on the fatal field of Waterloo.

But there is one aspect in which the Old Guard is not generally viewed—it did as much for human liberty as any army, from that of Gustavus Adolphus, down. I do not pretend to say how much the troops were governed by this motive—how many, or how few, fought solely for glory, but that Old Guard never made a charge, with the exception of the last, that did not give an impulse to human liberty. Every time it broke the ranks of the despots of Europe, armed against the free principles working in France, it wrenched a fetter from the human mind. In short, it carried the liberty of Europe on the points of its sabres. The wild waking up during the last few years is the working of the leaven of French principles, or rather I should say of American principles, sown by French hands. All honor, then, to the Old Guard for breaking up the iron frame-work of feudalism which had rusted so long in its place, that nothing but a stroke that should heave and rend everything asunder could affect its firmness.

As I said before, I do not ascribe the same motives to the Old Guard that existed in the hearts of the soldiers of the American army or Cromwell's troops. Still they err much, who deriving their ideas from English history, suppose that they had no definite idea of the struggle they were engaged in. The very fact that Napoleon cloaked his occupation of the Tuileries by calling on his Guard to wear crape for Washington, "who, like themselves, had fought against tyranny," shows how strongly rooted republican principles were in their hearts. They knew that hostilities were first commenced by the allied powers for the sole and undisguised purpose of destroying the French republic, and crushing the principles of freedom. They also well knew that the tremendous combinations that were constantly formed against France had no other object than to defend feudalism and establish the old order of things. All this the commonest soldier knew and talked about in his bivouac. The troops often stormed over intrenchments singing republican songs.

The continental monarchs also well understood the struggle, and foresaw what has since occurred—the uprising of the people, and the humiliation of royalty. The general, it is true, had become Emperor, but the code he gave the people bestowed on them all the freedom they knew how to use with safety to the government. Every proclamation Napoleon made to a conquered state, every change he proposed to a government, was an immense stride in the onward march of civil liberty. It was on this account his overthrow was sought with such eagerness. While he occupied the throne the old order of things threatened momentarily to disappear.

CHAPTER 13

The Guard After the Battle of Waterloo

The remains of the French army after the battle of Waterloo, fell back toward Paris whither the allies were already marching. The debris of the Old Guard were stationed in the environs to impose on the enemy, for the general belief was that the city would be defended. Since its last capture it had been strongly fortified and could now make a firm resistance. But the rout of the Old Guard had discouraged Paris more than the destruction of two armies would have done. The two chambers were thrown into the greatest agitation. Lafayette, in the Chamber of Deputies, offered a resolution calling on Napoleon to abdicate. At first the latter could not believe it would endeavor to dethrone him, but all men saw that France must wage an endless war, if she retained Napoleon, for nothing short of his overthrow would satisfy the allies. It was to gratify the wish of a disheartened nation that he finally consented to abdicate in favor of his son Napoleon II. But the army did not view things in the same way.

Two regiments of the Guard followed by a vast multitude, passed under the terrace of Elysée Bourbon, where Napoleon was, demanding with loud cries that their Emperor should put himself at their head, and conduct them against the enemy. Napoleon harangued them, urging them to quietness. An orator of the populace in replying to him mentioned the 18th Brumaire.

The Emperor interrupting him, exclaimed, "You recall to my remembrance the 18th Brumaire, but you forget that the circumstances are not the same. On the 18th Brumaire, the nation was unanimous in its desire of a change. A feeble effort only was necessary to effect what they so much desired. Now it would require oceans of French blood, and never shall a single drop be shed by me in the defence of a cause altogether personal."

Singular language for a tyrant. After all had dispersed, Montholon, who gives this account, expostulated with the Emperor for having arrested the hand of the people, strong enough in itself to save the capital from the enemy and punish the traitors who were negotiating to deliver it up. Napoleon replied in these words, which should be written in gold, and are sufficient of themselves to repel half the slanders his enemies have uttered against him. Note, he was speaking to an intimate friend in all the frankness of private intercourse.

"Putting the brute force of the people," said he, "into action, would doubtless save Paris and insure me the crown without incurring the horrors of civil war, but it would likewise be risking thousands of French lives, for what power could control so many various passions, so much hatred, and such vengeance! No, there is one thing you see I cannot forget, it is, that I have been escorted from Cannes to Paris amid the bloody cries of down with the priests! down with the nobles! No, I like the regrets of France better than her crown."

Noble words, uttered in a moment when his crown was leaving him, and nothing but the sad fate of an exile before him. The crown glittering on the one hand, together with the prospect of punishing his foes, banishment and disgrace on the other, and yet to say, "I like the regrets of. France better than her crown"—to say it too, when the saying was the doing, was the noblest proof that could be given of the truth he uttered. How strange it must sound to those who have contemplated him only by the light or rather darkness of English history, to hear this man whom they have regarded as a monster of cruelty, wading through seas of blood, refusing to save his crown, because in doing it, he must turn Frenchmen against Frenchmen. Ah, not one of his kingly foes would have done this—not one was ever heard to utter so noble a sentiment.

Napoleon having retired to Malmaison, General Beker was sent by the provisionary government to hasten his departure to America. While talking with him, the former asked, "Well, what are they saying and doing at Paris?" He replied, that opinions were very much divided about his abdication, "but the remnants of the army have remained faithful to you, and are assembled under the walls of the capital. A great proportion of the citizens and the whole people of Paris seem determined to defend themselves, and if a powerful hand could rally all these elements to a last effort, nothing would be hopeless perhaps." This plain hint thrown out by one who was sent to be his keeper, was lost on him, and he enquired only for his passports.

True enough the "remnants of the army were assembled under the walls of the capital," and there too, was the remnant of the Guard, still nearly twenty-six thousand strong, and filled with indignation at the decision to surrender Paris to the enemy. Officers and soldiers cried out treason, and uttered threats of vengeance. And when the order came to the battalions to abandon their post, they refused to obey. The old grenadiers broke their muskets and tore off their uniform, and cursed the authors of this great disgrace. Paris had fallen a year before, but had they been in its walls, the foot of the stranger would not have polluted its streets. So they and every one else had believed, and now to surrender it without striking a blow was a double disgrace, and an insult to their bravery.

Several officers protested against the capitulation, while the old veterans swore that before quitting the capital, they, at least, would take vengeance on the traitors, and thus do one act of justice. Brightened at the terrible aspect of these veterans, who were not yet humbled so low they could not strike boldly for their country, the generals of the army and the authorities prevailed on the favorite commanders of the Guard to intercede. Docile at the voice of their beloved Drouot and other favorite chiefs, they bowed in resignation. Being ordered beyond the Loire, where its tomb had already been prepared, it took up its sorrowful march. The bearing of all was mournful, but calm and resigned. Still the government was in constant terror lest Napoleon might again put himself at the head of his ancient braves, and sent Beker to hurry his embarkation.

While these things were passing at Paris, Napoleon was still at Malmaison, delaying his departure till the last moment. One morning, just before he was to set out, he was aroused by thundering shouts of "Vive l' Empereur, down with the Bourbons, down with the traitors." They arose from Bruyer's division which was returning from Vendee, where it had been stationed during the fatal Belgian campaign. The soldiers had halted before the chateau, refusing to take another step until the Emperor was at their head. The officers were compelled to submit, and General Bruyer went in and asked to see Napoleon. Montholon went in search of him, and found him in the library sitting by the window with his feet on the window sill, quietly reading Montaigne. While France was shaking to its centre, and his imperial crown lay broken at his feet, and the wrecks of his vast empire strewed the continent, and a desolate future stretched before him, he could compose himself and sit down quietly to his book, as if there was nothing to disturb the equanimity of his feelings.

General Bruyer was admitted, and in a quarter of an hour the army was on its march for Paris, shouting "Vive l' Empereur," in the full belief they should soon follow Napoleon to the field of battle.

Soon after, he sent a message to the government offering to take command of the army under Napoleon II., as a simple general, promising after he had repulsed the enemy, "to go to the United States, there to fulfil his destiny." In it he gave the plan he was to adopt, showed how feasible it was, and guaranteed that in a few days he would drive the enemy beyond the frontiers of France, and "avenge the disasters of Waterloo."

"Eighty thousand men, he said, "were gathering near Paris," which was "thirty thousand more than he had in the campaign of 1814." Although he then fought three months against the large armies of Russia, Austria, and Prussia; and France well knew that he would have been victorious in the struggle had it not been for the capitulation of Paris. It was moreover, 45,000 men more than General Bonaparte had headed when he crossed the Alps and conquered Italy." The government, instead of accepting the proposal, was terrified at it, and urged more vehemently than ever, his speedy departure.

Napoleon had not the slightest doubt his proposition would be accepted, and was preparing to take horse and join the army, when the refusal was brought him. Without exhibiting the least emotion, calm and serene as ever, he simply said, "Those people do not know the state of public opinion when they refuse my proposal; they will repent it," and added, "Give the necessary orders then for my departure, and as soon as everything is ready, let me know," and in an hour after, he was hurrying toward the sea shore.

"His forehead at this moment," says Montholon, "was sublime in its calmness and serenity."

Along the whole route to Rochefort, and after he arrived there, he was saluted with loud acclamations, and "Vive l' Empereur," heralded him to the coast where he committed the fatal mistake of trusting to the honor of the English government. He thought a great nation, like a great man, would be magnanimous, but discovered too late his error. Yet he was avenged on her, for the slow death and petty torture she inflicted upon him, was covered the laurels she won at Waterloo, with ashes.

In the meantime, the Old Guard had constantly urged Napoleon through messengers to put himself again at their head. They had followed him with their earnest request even to the sea-shore, but he steadily refused. Following quickly on the steps of this, came the order to disband the Guard. The soldiers were to be unmolested, but the officers who had served in the last campaign, were declared to be incapacitated to receive any title or to form a part of the new army about to be organised. Never before did a government give its own army so rude a blow. It might have been expected from an enemy, but for a corps that had covered France with glory and lifted her to an eminence she had never before reached, that had shed its blood freely for her protection, to be so disgraced by France itself, shows that the government was unworthy of such a noble phalanx.

Not content with executing this contemptible act, no sooner was the disbanding effected, than it commenced its proscription, and the superior officers were dragged before military commissioners. Ney, who led the last charge of the Old Guard, was publicly shot in violation of a sacred promise given by the allies, that he should be safe. At length the hatred of the king reached the inferior officers and they were designated "brigands of the Loire," and were forbidden to show themselves in Paris, or even occupy the localities which had been assigned them by the minister of war. They were hunted like deer up and down, and if one was heard to express the least regret over what had been done or recall a single souvenir of their ancient glory, he was immediately dragged before the provost court over which an old emigrant presided.

The officers finding there was no repose for them in France, sought refuge in foreign lands. Some went to Turkey, some to Greece, and others to different portions of the continent, where they were well received on account of their old renown. Some passed over to England, where help was extended them by noble men who sympathized with their misfortunes and honored them for their great deeds. Thus they became scattered up and down the earth, seeking a livelihood in various ways—many who had long held high commands, supporting themselves by teaching French. The officers of a corps composed of 26,000 men made a little army by themselves.

CHAMP D'ASILE

Many of the proscribed officers went to Spanish America and served in the war against Spain, while others came to the United States. Among these latter was the fiery Lefebvre Desnouettes, who had so often led the chasseurs of the Guard to the charge. Lallemand, one of Napoleon's bravest generals, came here also, and soon perceived that if these old warriors could not be rallied together in some one place, their characters would degenerate, and the French name, honored along our western rivers, suffer disgrace. A proscribed and exiled soldier descends by natural steps to the rank of an adventurer. He therefore planned a place of refuge for all, to be called the "Champ d' Asile." He finally selected a spot in Texas, about fifty miles above the mouth of Trinity river. He had two objects in view in this; first, to have a place to receive those officers who were exiled by the government, and those who voluntarily left the country to escape the persecutions they were subject to from the Bourbon dynasty, and in the second place, to establish a "propagande revolutionnaire," in the bosom of Mexico, or a society for the dissemination of free principles in the Spanish provinces, with the ultimate design of freeing Mexico from the Spanish yoke.

In 1817, General Lallemand, who had communicated to Joseph Bonaparte, then residing in Philadelphia, his plan, assembled the officers of the Guard, as well as the other proscribed officers of the army in that city. Having explained his intentions and expressed his hopes, he persuaded by his eloquence nearly all the inferior officers to accompany him. The general officers, however, thought the plan chimerical and unwise, and refused to join the enterprise, with the exception of the brave Rigaud, who fell in with it.

A ship was freighted with provisions for four or five hundred men, and six pieces of artillery, six hundred muskets, and a large supply of powder. Some days before their departure, Joseph Bonaparte gave to the more needy officers a sum of money sufficient to pay the debts they had contracted while in Philadelphia. He did not wish the officers of the Old Guard, those who had shared the fortunes and renown of his imperial brother, and borne through their long and glorious career so lofty a character, to have a spot, however slight, on their names.

The expedition, nearly two hundred strong, left Philadelphia the 17th of December, at seven o'clock in the morning, and arrived at Galveston Island the 18th of January. Here they disembarked to wait for Lallemand, and constructed huts of reeds and pieces of timber thrown ashore from shipwrecked vessels—surrounding the whole with a fosse—to protect their bivouac from the attacks of savages. On the 20th of March, Lallemand arrived with some sixty more, from New Orleans. Four days after, they started for the "Champ d'Asile," in ten large launches, which they had bought of a pirate.

The "Champ d'Asile," was a taking name—it spoke of rest and quiet after the troubled and wandering life of the last two years, but the spot itself was desolate enough. In those vast solitudes surrounded by wild beasts and rattlesnakes and implacable Indians, these veteran officers of the Old Guard were to make themselves a home. To dishearten them still more, the fleet of boats which on their arrival they had sent back after the provisions, remained absent a month.

The exiles, however, put on a cheerful countenance, and commenced their organization. Three cohorts of infantry, cavalry, and artillery, were formed to defend the colony and maintain orders while fortifications were erected to protect them from the attacks of the Spaniards and Indians. The last time those officers had superintended the erection of fortifications, was on some great battle-field of Europe; now they were laboring with their own hands in the wilds of Texas. Their camp was guarded with the same scrupulous care they were wont to guard their bivouac, when Napoleon was in their midst. Then all were officers, while now all but a few ranked as common soldiers. This little army of officers spent a good deal of its time in manœuvring and military exercises.

For the generals, superior officers, and women, large huts were constructed, but all the others bivouacked as they did in Poland, during the campaigns of Eylau and Friedland, eating their meals from wooden trenchers. To drive away wild animals an enormous fire, made of fallen trees, was kept constantly burning, around which, at all hours of the day, groups of veterans could be seen telling stories of the past and awakening the memory of by-gone deeds of fame. The environs of the fire these exiles jocosely called the Palais Royal, and those who told stories and related adventures, the fops that promenaded it.

Lallemand would often come to this "Palais Royal," and relate conversations he had had with Napoleon in the closing up of his career. In the forests of Russia and in many a desolate spot those exiles had ordered just such a fire built in the midst of their squares, and now as they recalled those scenes, they could almost see the form of Napoleon standing before it, as he was wont to do, with his hands crossed behind him and his stern brow knit in deep thought. The past came back with renewed freshness. Each one had some reminiscence of his chief—so, said one, did he stand before our fire on the morning of the battle of Dresden, and never moved, while the thunder of cannon was shaking the field; and so, said another, did we surround him in the forest of Minsk, on the banks of the Beresina.

They traversed the whole ground from Lodi and Arcola, to Waterloo, fighting all their battles over again, and then their eyes would gleam as they spoke of St. Helena. It was a singular spectacle to behold those veterans from the pyramids, from Marengo, from Austerlitz, Jena, Eylau, and Borodino, grouped together around a huge fire in the forests of Texas, recounting their deeds and making the woods echo with shouts of *"Vive l' Empereur."*

One could hardly believe that they had passed through such great and stirring scenes for nearly a quarter of a century, and that those poor exiles had led the columns of the Old Guard in its terrible onsets, and that their shout of victory had gone up from the greatest battle-fields of Europe. It looked strange to see in that far- off temple of verdure, the eagle of Austerlitz lifted on high, and around it grouped the symbols and trophies they had preserved with religious care.

But no description can give such a vivid impression of the whole scene, as the celebrated picture of Horace Vernet, called the "Soldat Laboreur," in which he exhibits in all the distinctness of life the old soldier of the Imperial Guard—his face seamed with scars—the cross of honor on his breast, and his spade in his hand toiling in the solitudes of Texas.

Thus they passed weeks and months in their solitary home making the woods ring with the stirring description of marches, and sieges, and battles, and victories. Some among them had been with Napoleon at Elba, and recalled his kindness to his Old Guard there, and how cheerful he seemed when manœuvring his little band, as though it were the grand army.

They had long conversations about him in his island prison, and spent much of their time in forming plans to effect his deliverance. One was, to obtain a swift sailing ship, and hover round the coast till a favorable opportunity offered itself, and then make a sudden descent and carry him off. If that remnant of the Old Guard could once have set foot on the island, it would have required something more than bayonets to have stopped their march on Longwood. But what did they design to do with him when they had effected his release? To go to France and exhibit another return from Elba, and another triumphal entry into Paris? No, they "would bring him to the Champ d'Asile." He should stand before their bivouac fire, as of old, and they would minister to his wants and he would be content in their midst. What a hold he must have had upon their affections when he could fill them with such desperate resolutions and longing desire to have him with them.

But sickness soon began to thin their ranks and break down their hopes. In the meantime, the Mexican government having learned that a French colony had, without permission, settled upon its territory, sent a detachment of twelve hundred men to destroy it.

The Indians, who had ever been friendly to the exiles, informed them of the premeditated attack. The latter immediately put themselves in a posture of defence, determined, notwithstanding their inferiority of numbers, to maintain their ground. The Spanish commander, however, halted when within three marches of their camp, and waited for sickness and discouragement to do what he dared not attempt.

He was not compelled to wait long. Not receiving the means they expected from France, to carry out their plan of freeing Mexico, and finding that after the first excitement had passed away, the Champ d'Asile had become in their country a subject of ridicule rather than of serious thought, and no assistance could be expected from any source, they resolved to abandon the colony. Their numbers were constantly diminishing, and it was madness to stay till their weakness would render them an easy prey to whomsoever might attack them.

On the 6th of August, therefore, or a little more than four months from the time they landed, they abandoned their camp and went over to Galveston Island. They remained here a month longer, when, to complete their wretchedness, a horrible tempest swept the gulf. The waves rose to an immense height, rolling several feet deep over the island. These weary veterans, as they looked out on the wide waste of water, gave themselves up for lost. But there chanced to be two large and strongly-built cabins situated some distance from the shore which offered a temporary protection, and they crowded into them. Here for three days and nights they struggled manfully against the waves,-

when the storm subsided. Their provisions and powder, however, were all swallowed up in the sea. Their ammunition was their last hope, but it had gone like all their other hopes, since the battle of Waterloo.

Another month of agony was endured on this island, at the expiration of which General Lallemand sent word that all prospect of attaining the end they had in view was gone, and requested them to return to New Orleans. The same pirate that had before carried them to the island took them off. The sick and feeble went by water, but the stronger crossed over to the mainland, and guided by the Indians, struck through the forests of Texas to the frontiers of Louisiana, where many of them stopped and repaid the hospitality they received by teaching the children French. Those who went to New Orleans reached there just as the yellow fever was raging with the greatest violence, and they, one after another, fell before its fury.

Fifteen months after, a subscription of 80,000 francs, which had been collected in France, was received. But between the sea, sickness, yellow fever, and accidents, the ranks of those brave officers had become sadly thinned, so that out of more than two hundred, only forty-seven could be found. Those, with their usual generosity, divided the money with those who had been drawn to New Orleans by false promises, but had not yet embarked for the "Champ d' Asile."

The artillery of the enemy did not thin the ranks of the Old Guard faster than proscription, exile, poverty, and disease. Those who came to this country disappeared like snow.

Once more only, do we get a glimpse of the Old Guard. A large number of wounded and maimed soldiers were in the Hotel des Invalides when the body of Napoleon was brought back from St. Helena, "to rest," as he requested in his will, "on the banks of the Seine, amid the people he loved." These dressed in the old uniform of chasseurs, grenadiers, &c., came forth to receive him. Amid the pomp and funereal splendor of that day, nothing moved the people more than the appearance of these invalid soldiers as they stood on each side of the entrance of the church to receive the body of their old chieftain. The last time they saw him was on the field of battle, and now the waving of standards and thunder of cannon, recalled the days when he marched in their midst. The past came back in such a sudden and overwhelming tide when they saw the coffin approach, that struck dumb with grief, they fell on their knees and stretched out their hands towards it, while tears rolled silently down their scarred visages.

Long after, he who visited the Hotel des Invalides at any hour of the day would see these old soldiers treading softly around the coffin of Napoleon, as though they were afraid to disturb his repose. That elevated tomb at night presented an imposing spectacle; upon the pall that covered this strange and mighty being, lay his hat worn at Eylau, his sword and his crown, while over all mournfully drooped the standards taken at Austerlitz. In the centre of the gold-bordered draperies that extended from column to column of the chapel, shone in large letters, MARENGO, WAGRAM, AUSTERLITZ, JENA. A chandelier, suspended from the ceiling, shed a dim light over all. Around this tomb, night and day, stood four veterans with drawn sabres, and often on the steps that led to it, you would see a mutilated grenadier of the Old Guard kneeling as if in prayer.

Such is the history, and such was the character of the Old Guard, "a phalanx of giants," the like of which the world has never beheld. Its fame will deepen with time, and its memory grow dearer to all those who honor great deeds and noble men.

CHAPTER 14

The Return of the Emperor

In 1836, when the body of Napoleon was brought back from St. Helena, the magnificent arch of triumph which terminates the grand avenue of the Champs Elysées, in Paris, was for the first time dedicated. Frederick Soulier has taken advantage of this coincidence to write a long article entitled "A Review of the Dead."

After the myriad lamps that lighted all the avenues of the magnificent grounds of the Champs Elysées during the evening of the celebration, had been extinguished, and the tread of the vast multitude, and the hum of their voices, had given place to the silence and darkness of night, a sound like the passing wing of an eagle was heard sweeping by, and lo, a colossal shade stood on the top of the arch of triumph. It was that of Napoleon wrapped in the blue mantle that folded him on the night after the battle of Marengo.

As he stood and surveyed the scene, he called to his side the shade of his son, and then summoned from their distant fields of fame his vast and slumbering armies from Egypt, from Palestine, from Italy, from Spain, from the snow-drifts of Russia and the glaciers of the Alps, from Marengo, and Austerlitz, and Jena, and Wagram, and Friedland, and Leipsic, and Waterloo, the dead armies, headed by their respective leaders, came forth and marched silently and swiftly forward. As they approached the vault of the arch under which they were to pass, Napoleon pointed out each brave leader to his son. Kleber and Desaix, and Lannes bearing the banner of Lodi and the sabre of honor of Marengo, and Augereau, with the flag that he carried through the tempest of fire that swept the bridge of Arcola, Lefebvre, and the two Kellermans and the brave Massena, each followed by their tens of thousands passed in succession, their shadowy footfalls giving back no echo.

As column after column swept under the arch, the colossal shade on the top cried out, "close up your ranks and press forward, for the morning approaches, and I wish to see you all before the day dawns." The brave grenadiers marched up, followed as was their wont in the desperate charge, by the thundering squadrons of Bessieres. Murat, on his prancing steed, came after, stooping as he bounded beneath the vault, as though his plume would reach the lofty arch. Poniatowsky, and Rapp, and last of all, Ney, the bravest of the brave, without arms, pale, and pierced with wounds received on no battle-field, moved by with their thousands, and the pageant was over. But before they disappeared, the colossal shade stooped and pointed with his sword to the arch. A sudden flash of lightning illuminated the sides, and there these heroes saw their names inscribed in imperishable rock.

With the first streakings of dawn in the east, the vast and shadowy host disappeared.

The sentinel on watch that night at the entrance of the arch, said that all night long the wind groaned and swept in strange whispers through the trees of the Champs Elysées and the vault of the arch. It was the swift marching of the ghostly columns in this "review of the dead."

Could such a marshalling of the hosts of Napoleon take place, what a spectacle would be presented. Before the amazing scenes that would rise one after another in rapid succession, the mind and senses would be overwhelmed.

But there is another review, though not appealing to the senses, which is still more startling and terrific—a review embracing the progress of civil freedom, which marched with those iron columns, whose heavy footsteps sounded the death-knell of tyranny in all Europe—the waking up of the human mind from the sleep of ages, to think and act for itself—the rending of fetters—the sudden daylight poured on man's oppressions—the breaking up of old systems—the upheaving of thrones—the development of moral power, and the final launch of the world, with all its hopes and interests, upon the turbulent sea of democracy.

In my "Napoleon and his Marshals," I gave a succinct review of the relations the former sustained to the nations of Europe, fixing the guilt of the wars he waged with such fierceness on the governments that surrounded him. Having since observed that those who differed with me took those statements as mere assertions, I shall be pardoned for devoting the last chapter of this work to proofs of what I then said, in order to show that while describing his deeds, and those of his Guard, I have not been eulogizing mere warriors, fighting only for renown, but men engaged the greater part of the time in the cause of freedom.

In the first place, no one who professes to give an opinion on history denies that the first coalition against France was without the least provocation. The people chose to get rid of the Bourbons and establish a republic, and the allied powers chose they should not. Their only pretence for going to war against a nation with which they were at peace, was, that a republic endangered the tranquillity of Europe, and the stability of their thrones. They considered this an ample reason and needing no defence, and so France was assailed on every side.

As we, in both our wars with England, directed our efforts at once against Canada, so did France move against the Austrian possessions in Italy, and for the same reason, viz., because she could more easily reach her enemy there. The only difference in the two cases is, that we, especially in 1812, waged what some might term an offensive war, while that of the republic was entirely a defensive one. Therefore, as general of the French army in Italy, Bonaparte did nothing more than obey his government, while his government, in assailing its enemy, did that which no one can for a moment condemn. Hence, it is not difficult to designate the authors of these bloody wars.

But after defeating the Austrians, it is said he marched into Rome, and treated a neutral power as an enemy, for the sole love of conquest. Let us look at the facts: Under the mediation of Spain, an armistice had been concluded with the Papal States, at Bologna, and ratified at Rome. But Cardinal Busca, who succeeded Cardinal Zelada as Secretary of State, repudiated this armistice, and openly formed a connection with Austria, with which France was at war, and attempted to raise an army.

Having chosen to break his plighted word, and become an enemy to the republic, the Pope could not expect otherwise than to share the fate of an enemy. As good fortune would have it, the courier sent from Rome to Vienna with despatches announcing this alliance, was intercepted near Mezzolo. These despatches declared that the "armistice of Bologna would not be executed, notwithstanding the loud complaints of the French minister, Cacault—that the Pope was raising troops, and that he had accepted the commander-in-chief proposed by Austria, and requested that general to bring with him a good number of officers, engineers, and artillery." Cacault, of course, was ordered by the French government to leave Rome at once, and Napoleon marched into the capital of his Holiness. With regard to the levies he made on the Pope for thus violating the armistice, and allying himself with an enemy, I have nothing to say, for my purpose is not to defend a single action of Napoleon, as a man or a ruler, except it relates to the simple question of peace and war. I wish only to show on whose shoulders rests the responsibility of those terrific wars which we have so long charged to Bonaparte, and which make it seem so criminal in any one to defend him.

The campaign in Egypt which followed, was undertaken entirely for conquest. Russia had the north and most of the west of Asia; England possessed the south; and Bonaparte declared that France should claim the Levant. The expedition was based on the self-same motives which prompted England to wage an aggressive war in India, and the United States in Mexico; and no reasonable mind would ever adduce it, except to prove that France, like all other nations, desired colonies, and was not very scrupulous about the method of obtaining them.

We now come to the appointment of Bonaparte as First Consul. After his elevation to the head of affairs, he was responsible for the acts of government; for he was, in fact, the government, long before he placed on his head the imperial crown.

His first act, on assuming the direction of affairs, was noble, and clears him triumphantly from the charge of being the author of the war that followed. Stepping aside from the usual path of diplomacy, he wrote, with his own hand, two letters—one to the king of England, and another to the emperor of Germany. To the first, he said:

Called, Sire, by the wishes of the French nation, to occupy the first magistracy of the Republic, I judge it well, on entering my office, to address myself directly to your majesty.

Must the war which, for the last eight years, has devastated the four quarters of the world, be eternal? Are there no means of coming to an understanding? How can the two most enlightened nations of Europe, stronger already and more powerful than their safety or their independence requires, sacrifice, to the ideas of vain-glory, the well-being of commerce, internal prosperity, and the peace of families? How is it that they do not feel peace to be the first of necessities as the first of glories?

These sentiments cannot be strangers to the heart of your majesty, who governs a free people, with the sole aim of rendering it happy.

Your majesty will perceive only in this overture the sincerity of my desire to contribute efficaciously, for the second time, to a general pacification by this prompt advance, perfectly confidential and disembarrassed of those forms, which, perhaps necessary to disguise the dependence of weak states, reveal, when adopted by strong states, only the wish of mutual deception.

France and England, by the misuse of their powers, may yet, for a long period, retard, to the misery of all nations, their own exhaustion. But I venture to say that the fate of all civilized nations is connected with the termination of a war which has set the whole world in flames.

Bonaparte
First Consul of the French Republic

He wrote at the same time to the emperor of Germany, the following letter:

Having returned to Europe after an absence of eighteen months, I find a war kindled between the French Republic and your majesty.

The French nation has called me to the occupation of the first magistracy.

A stranger to every feeling of vain-glory, the first of my wishes is, to stop the effusion of blood which is about to flow. Everything leads me to foresee that in the next campaign, numerous armies, well conducted, will treble the number of victims who have already fallen since the resumption of hostilities. The well known character of your majesty leaves me no doubt as to the secret wishes of your heart. If those wishes are only listened to, I perceive the possibility of reconciling the interests of the two nations.

In the relations which I have formerly entertained with your majesty, you have shown me some personal regard; I beg you, therefore, to see in this overture, which I have made to you, the desire to respond to that regard, and to convince your majesty more and more of the very distinguished consideration which I feel towards you.

Bonaparte

Here was a frank and generous challenge to peace, made in all sincerity, to two nations which had so long waged an unprovoked war against France. The king of England would not condescend to reply directly, but sent an answer through his minister; and instead of meeting these advances towards a pacification, he made out a long list of charges against France, accusing the Republic of violent and oppressive acts, declaring that in the present change of the government he saw no guarantee for the future—in short, that nothing could satisfy his majesty but the restoration of the house of Bourbon.

The whole reply was weak and ridiculous, and was so regarded by sensible men at the time. Bonaparte, instead of yielding to indignation, replied in courteous terms. Reviewing the past, he proved conclusively that France took up arms solely to resist an aggressive war, made on her by Europe banded together to overthrow the Republic; and while he did not deny that acts of violence had been committed, he more than hinted that they who had attacked France with such animosity; should look to themselves as the cause of them. "But," he added, "to what good end are all these reminiscences? Here is now a government well disposed to put an end to war. Is the war to be eternal, because this or that party was the first aggressor? And if it be not desired to render it eternal, must there not be first an end made of these endless recriminations? At all events, if they could not make a peace at once, let them agree on an armistice and give time and facilities for coming to a good understanding."

Lord Grenville, the English minister, seeing the ridiculous and unpleasant attitude in which Bonaparte had placed him, replied in worse temper and worse reasoning than before, and finally confessed that England waged war "for the securityof all governments," and no offers of peace would be listened to.

Austria replied in a more becoming manner, and for once was perfectly honest, for she declared that "war was carried on, only to preserve Europe from a general earthquake." "The security of all governments," and the prevention of "a general earthquake," meant the same thing, namely, the destruction of a mighty republic that had arisen from under a throne in the midst of their thrones. Bonaparte, of course, understood the import of this language—it was saying emphatically, "We do not want peace; we will not even entertain a proposition for it until the republic is no more." Fox, Sheridan, Lord Holland, and others, bore down with tremendous power on this decision of the British government.

"You ask," said they, "who was the aggressor? and what matters that? You say that it is France, and France says that it is England. Is it then necessary to maintain an internecine war until both nations shall agree on a point of history. And what matters it who is the aggressor, if that party which is accused thereof be the first which offers to lay down its arms! You say it is useless to treat with France. Yet yourselves sent Lord Malmsbury to Lille to treat with the Directory. Prussia and Spain have treated with the French Republic, and have had no cause for complaint. You speak of ambition, but Russia, Prussia, and Austria, have divided Poland. Austria has reconquered Italy without restoring to their states the princes dispossessed by France. Either you will never treat at all with the French Republic, or you will never find a more favorable moment for doing so. Unless it be confessed that Great Britain, her blood, her treasure, all her resources, the most precious, are to be wasted for the re-establishment of the house of Bourbon, no good reason can be assigned why we should now refuse to treat"

Tierney, also, hit the government to the quick—said he, "Do you remember the war with America? Is it not rather for the principle it represents you are striving."

Sheridan referring to the capitulation to Brune, of the late English expedition against Holland, said, "It seems that if our government cannot conclude treaties of peace with the French republic, it can at least conclude capitulations."

Bonaparte forced into a war, soon made Europe tremble with the tread of his legions. The battles of Engen and Maeskirk, Ulm, Genoa, Montibello, crowned with the terrible slaughter of Marengo, rest not on Bonaparte, nor on the French Republic, but on England and Austria, which refused even to negotiate for peace. From this last battlefield, Bonaparte, deeply affected by the spectacle it presented, wrote again a long letter to the emperor of Austria. Forgetting, in the impulse of the moment, the ceremonious forms of diplomacy, he said:

It is on the field of battle, amid the sufferings of a multitude of the wounded, and surrounded by 15,000 corpses, that I beseech your majesty to listen to the voice of humanity, and not to suffer two brave nations to cut each other's throats for interests not their own. It is my part to press this on your majesty, being upon the very theatre of war. Your majesty's heart cannot feel it so keenly as does mine." After the first emotions had subsided, he felt somewhat mortified that he had given way to such impulsive expressions to men who calculated everything by the cold rules of diplomacy, and in speaking of the letter to the consuls, he told them with an air of chagrin, they "might think it somewhat original, but it was written on the field of battle.

An armistice followed, and so anxious was Bonaparte to contract a treaty of peace, that the Austrian minister at Paris was persuaded to sign articles conditionally, although he was not empowered to do so.

But this long armistice wore away without any definite results, and the campaign of Hohenlinden followed. Austria, now thoroughly alarmed, agreed to sign a peace immediately, although the terms insisted on by Bonaparte were much harder than those he had induced the Austrian minister during the armistice to sign conditionally. It is true France acquired territory by this treaty, and she had a right to do so. Austria could expect nothing else from a nation it had forced into a war. The great expense and sacrifice necessary to secure the marvelous victories which had saved France, demanded some reward. It is worthy of remark here, that all the possessions Bonaparte obtained, were given up by treaty to compensate for an unjust and aggressive war. This was the peace of Luneville, signed the 9th of February, 1801. I will say nothing of the conditions of that treaty, whether hard on the allies or not. Whatever they might think of them, they had themselves only to thank.

Both England and Austria at last discovered that they could treat with the French Republic, for it began to dawn on them that while fighting for the security of other governments, they might not be able to take care of their own.

In October of this year, the celebrated peace of Amiens was concluded, and Europe was at rest. Among other conditions in this treaty, England was to evacuate Egypt and Malta, and France evacuate Naples, Tarento, and the Roman States. Bonaparte carried out his part of the treaty in two months, while ten months passed away and England took no steps to evacuate Malta and Egypt. When pressed to execute the terms of a solemn treaty she shuffled and procrastinated until at length the First Consul's interference in the affairs of Switzerland gave her a pretext for her refusal. Revolution and counter-revolution were wrecking the Swiss Confederacy, and Bonaparte, called upon for help, marched his troops to the frontiers, and put down the oligarchs. The expeditions and just manner in which he settled the difficulties, brought forth warm congratulations from both the Russian and Prussian cabinets. England was astonished to see the only available excuse for violating a treaty taken from her hands, but remained stubborn to her purpose.

At length Bonaparte put the question categorically to the English minister, Lord Whitworth:

> Will you or will you not execute the treaty of Amiens? I have executed it on my part with scrupulous fidelity. That treaty obliged me to evacuate Naples,

Tarento, and the Roman States within three months, in less than two all the French troops were out of those countries. Ten months have elapsed since the exchange of the ratifications and the English troops are still in Malta and at Alexandria. It is useless to try to deceive us on this point; will you have peace, or will you have war?

He declared that he would not see that solemn treaty violated—it would disgrace the French nation and prove her incapable of defending her honor. "For my part," said he, "my resolution is fixed; I had ratherseeyou in possession of the heights of Montmartre than of Malta." He wound up by saying:

> Now, if you doubt my desire to preserve peace, listen, and judge how far I am sincere. Though yet very young, I have attained a renown to which it would be difficult to add. Do you imagine I am willing to risk this power in a desperate struggle? But if I have a war with Austria, I will contrive to find my way to Vienna. If I have a war with you, I will take from you every ally on the continent.

In this frank manner he went on declaring what he wished and what he would do, if forced again into a war, saying—that if England was bent on perpetual war, he would endeavor to cross the straits, "and, perhaps, bury in the depths of the sea his fortune, his glory, and his life." He strained every nerve to preserve the peace, and even endeavored to compromise the matter, by offering to put Malta into the hands of the Emperor of Russia in trust, until the differences between France and England could be settled. Nothing, however, would do; England was bent on a rupture, and Bonaparte seeing that all his efforts were useless, said:

Henceforth the treaties must be covered with black crape." On the 20th of May, 1803, he issued a proclamation declaring the rupture of the treaty of Amiens. No one acquainted with history doubts on whom the guilt of involving Europe in the war that followed, and of deluging her plains in blood rests. Even Alison, a high tory English writer, and who never loses an opportunity to exculpate his country on the most frivolous pleas, is compelled to hold the following remarkable language: "In coolly reviewing the circumstances under which this contest was renewed, it is impossible to deny that the Britishgovernmentmanifested a feverish anxiety to come to a rupture, and that so far as the two countrieswere concerned, they were the aggressors."

Bonaparte immediately prepared for war, and the invasion of England occupied all his thoughts. In the meantime, however, the Emperor of Russia offered his mediation, which Napoleon at once accepted, and proposed to make him "sole arbiter of the great quarrel which occupied the world." He even promised "to give a bond by which he would engage to submit to the award of the Emperor Alexander, whatever it might be, confided entirely in his justice."

England knowing the injustice of her cause, refused to make Alexander supreme judge in the case, but had no objections to use him as an agent, which she endeavored to do. This Bonaparte resented, and abruptly abandoned the project.

Alexander, however, young, ambitious, and giddy, became persuaded that it devolved on him to settle the affairs of the continent A plan was therefore set on foot for the reconstruction of Europe. This plan contained many generous features and many whimsical ideas. When submitted to the English government it was shorn of its visionary portions and despoiled of its generosity. It was, however, a god-send to England, for by her superior diplomacy she made it the groundwork of a new coalition against France. I cannot go into the history of this coalition. After many alterations and long discussions, &c., a plan was formed which proposed three things:

1. To cut down France to her former limits before the revolution. To take away from her all she had gained in a defensive war, and which had been secured to her by treaty with these very powers. Its first object, therefore, was the same as if the allied powers should now combine to take from us the territory recently ceded to us by Mexico. The only difference in the two cases would be that France won her possessions in resisting aggression, and her domination was preferred by the people themselves; while we gained ours by an unprovoked war, and forced unwilling subjects to submit to our authority.

2. To dispose of all the weaker states as the allies thought proper, without any reference to the wishes of the states themselves. Austria and Prussia, which would be compelled to bear the brunt of the struggle, they knew must reap some decided advantage from the coalition, or they would not join it. Lombardy was, therefore, promised to Austria, and all the Low Countries to Prussia, while the Republics of Italy which Napoleon had formed should be parcelled out to different sovereigns. A more villainous transaction could not have been concocted. Its aim, of course, was to extinguish all the independent states governed by free principles which Napoleon had set up and defended.

The last proposition was in general terms, thrown in as a saving clause to cover all their transactions—it was "to establish a system of public right throughout Europe." This "public right" meant security against republican principles. Bonaparte, in resisting the aggressive war of Austria, conquered her possessions in Italy, and had a perfect right to incorporate them into France. But this he refused to do, and instead, erected them into a republic. It was not the conquests that Bonaparte was making that alarmed the sovereigns of Europe, but the independent republics he formed from the possessions he wrung from the enemy, and to which that enemy could show no title. These republics, all looking to the powerful arm of Napoleon for protection, were like so many ghosts to monarchs, standing and pointing at their thrones.

This coalition, called the third, which, in the end, was to cover Europe with the slain, progressed slowly, and seemed averse to enter on the dreadful struggle without some excuse to conceal the real motives that swayed it. At length that excuse was found in the incorporation of Genoa and the Cis-Alpine Republic into the French Empire. The 11th article of the treaty of Luneville says, "The contracting parties shall mutually guarantee the independence of Batavia, the Helvetian, Cis-Alpine, and Ligurian Republics, and the right to the people who inhabit them to adopt whatever formofgovernment they think fit." The merging of these Italian republics, therefore, was declared a violation of that treaty and a sufficient cause for war.

Look at the honesty of the pretence here set up. A year before this took place, these same upholders of sacred treaties had formed the plan to give Holland to Prussia, as a bribe for her cooperation; Lombardy, to Austria; and the Ligurian Republic to Sardinia. After having deliberately resolved to quench these free States, which they had guaranteed to preserve, they had the audacity to declare that the merging of them into the French Empire was the cause of the coalition.

Certainly if these republics were to disappear as independent governments, they belonged to France. She had conquered them and refrained originally from incorporating them into her, because she preferred to make them free. More than this, who could blame Napoleon when he saw a vast conspiracy forming against him, the plan of which he could not get at, for strengthening himself on every side? This young and enthusiastic ruler had dreamed in his ambition, of reconstructing society, of advancing civil freedom and waking up men to new views and hopes, and for this purpose had made republics out of conquered states. But now he looked around him and saw the strongest monarchies of Europe concerting together for his overthrow. With whom could he combine to resist them—with what powers could he form an alliance?

There was nothing left to sympathise with him but those grateful young republics, and who could blame him for wishing their aid to stay up his empire? Any monarch threatened as he was, would have done it. But the infamous coalition had not even this excuse. By that very article of the treaty of Luneville it was guaranteed "to the people the right to adopt whatever form of government they thought fit," and that right they exercised in choosing that of the French Empire. Napoleon did not incorporate these republics into his empire—he did not subvert the free governments he had given them.

The Cis-Alpine Republic and Genoa, separately, in Legislature assembled, passed a decree requesting to be taken into that Empire. They saw a coming storm and avoided it in the best way they could. Separately, they could do nothing against a coalition. They would be wiped out with a single blow. Holland was to be given to Prussia; why should not she prefer to ally herself with France which had restored her independence? The Cis-Alpine Republic was to go back to the dreaded and hated domination of Austria; why should she not prefer the sway of Napoleon, when he guaranteed to her free laws? Genoa was to be handed over to the tyrannical king of Sardinia; how could she do otherwise than ask the protection of the French eagles? All these states saw that trouble was brewing, and they knew whatever shape it took, the success of the allies would ensure their overthrow. No alternative, therefore, was left them, and as they had a right to choose their own form of government, they of course had the right also to choose their relations to France.

That Napoleon, when he saw the drift of things, desired and sought the incorporation of these separate republics into his empire, no one doubts. France had changed into a monarchy, and a corresponding change would naturally pass over those who relied for safety on her protection; still no violence or threats were used.

The senate of Genoa, by a vote of twenty out of twenty-two, resolved to ask to be incorporated into the French Empire in order to partake of its fortunes and enjoy its prosperity. This vote, before being executed, was submitted to the people. Registers were opened, and the people called upon to give their suffrages on the question. The majority in favor of the incorporation was overwhelming. Lucca sent the same request, but Napoleon refused, and made it instead a separate principality.

The Cis-Alpine, or, as it had become, the Italian Republic, through its vice-president, Count Melzi, asked of the French Senate to be incorporated into the Empire, declaring "it saw no other way of saving its infant institutions." The Vice President then read "the fundamental articles of the act of settlement by which Napoleon was declared King of Italy."

Holland, though long ago conquered by the French, was still a free state, though a close ally of France, and bound by treaty to share her fortunes. As the final disappearance of this old commonwealth into a monarchy, with a brother of Napoleon at its head, has often been bitterly denounced, it may not be amiss to glance at its history. For a long succession of years the Netherlands were divided into two parties, Orange and anti-Orange. Without referring to other differences, it is necessary for our purpose to state only that the anti-Orange was the republican party. These two factions strove against each other with various successes till 1747, when the Orange party triumphed and the dignity of Stadtholder was made hereditary in the family of William IV. In 1786, however, the republicans again obtained the ascendancy and drove the Stadtholder out of the provinces. But Prussia coming to the rescue with 25,000 men, the Orange party was reinstated in power.

The French Revolution followed, and when in 1794 the republican army approached the frontiers of Holland, the patriots again rose, and with its aid, overthrew the hereditary Stadtholder. A republic was immediately formed after the model of that of France. The result was, Great Britain declared war against her and robbed her of some of her most valuable colonies, and nearly destroyed her commerce and finances. This is the famous conquest of Holland by France. She put an end to her internal troubles, and gave her a free and independent government, while England, which declaimed so loudly against the rapacity of the new republic, robbed her of her territory as unscrupulously as she has since robbed India of her possessions.

It was owing to the bankruptcy which England had caused that compelled her at length to seek admission into the French Empire. In view of the evils that embarrassed the state, the states- general sent four ambassadors to Paris, who declared that Holland saw no escape from bankruptcy, and requested, as a favor, to be incorporated into the empire. "They even proffered to let their debt remain chargeable upon themselves and to make every exertion to pay, provided they were no longer called upon to submit to a greater amount of taxation than the French. These ambassadors remained four months in Paris and were finally authorised to offer the crown to Louis. "We come," said they, "of our own accord and supported by nine-tenths of the suffrages of our fellow countrymen to entreat you to unite your fate with ours, and to raise a whole people from the perils with which they are threatened." Napoleon was compelled to command before he could induce his brother to accept the crown. So much for the destruction of this ancient commonwealth, brought about by British avarice and not French ambition. But this fusion of the republic into that of France did not take place till long after the coalition I have been speaking of. At that time it was independent and sustained no relation to France, except that of an ally.

Although the offer of this commonwealth could not bribe Prussia into the coalition formed by England and Russia, the latter promised to precipitate secretly a large army upon her frontier, under the pretence of protecting her, which should, and did prove a conclusive argument. Austria, however, voluntarily came into it, and the campaign of Austerlitz followed. For the bloody battles that were only preparatory to the crowning slaughter at Austerlitz, who is responsible? Not Napoleon, not France but the coalition. The treaty of Presbourg immediately succeeded this brilliant victory, and Austria and France were at peace. Russia, Prussia, and England, however, maintained the contest, and the campaigns of Jena, Eylau, and Friedland, followed—all the sad results of this infamous coalition, which Napoleon, however, with his terrific blows broke into a thousand fragments. The peace of Tilsit again put the continental powers at peace, but England feeling safe in her isolated position, still maintained her belligerent attitude.

The troubles with Spain succeeded this interregnum of war. I shall not attempt to defend this invasion, although viewed through the medium of European diplomacy there is much that might be said in palliation of Napoleon's conduct. His entrance into Spain was welcomed by the intelligent portion of the realm as calculated to put an end to the internal troubles and the weak government under which they suffered. Napoleon was not so much deceived by the representations made him, as many suppose. Joseph would have been welcomed by the strength of the nation, and the partial resistance soon have ceased, but for the interference and encouragement of England.

But granting all that the bitterest enemy may say of Napoleon's conduct towards Spain, which all things considered, is doubtless very like our treatment of Mexico, what shall we say of the authors of the campaigns of Abensberg, Landshut, Eckmuhl, Aspern, and Wagram, and at whose doors shall we lay the guilt of covering Europe with mangled and bleeding hosts? Thus far history is plain and the testimony of candid historians, although enemies, harmonise in one conclusion.

Even the uncandid are compelled to resort to the ridiculous assertion that the allies were justified in their course, because they foresaw clearly the mounting ambition of Napoleon. It was necessary to check at once this ambitious spirit that otherwise would ride over Europe. It is an old proverb, "there is no reasoning against prophecy." It is always the resort of a weak cause. But still unprejudiced men will think that to create a war in order to prevent one—to set Europe in a blaze to keep it from taking fire, is rather a novel mode of proceeding. Besides, to punish a person in advance because he may do wrong, to hang a man to prevent him from committing murder, or cast him into a prison because he shows a strong tendency to steal, would be considered a very singular mode of administrating law. If this mode of reasoning can be justified, the original holy alliance has now a perfect right to demand Kossuth and chain him to a rock in the midst of the ocean, as it did Napoleon, because his freedom endangers, in their opinion, the peace of Europe, and in case of refusal on our part, to declare war against us. Certainly if the reasoning is ever good that England and Russia, without one foot of their territory being violated, have a right to form a coalition against all independent power because they think the "security of Europe" requires it, they have that right now, and it makes no difference whether it be France or America which is to be struck.

Leaving Spain with all the obloquy and wrong attached to its invasion without a word of excuse, what, as I said before, shall be said of the new war that followed in Germany. The ruddy fields of Abensberg, Landshut, Eckmuhl, Aspern, and Wagram covered with mangled men cry out for vengeance against some one. Who violated the treaty of Presbourg, Napoleon or the Emperor of Austria? The former was in Spain with his army, far removed from any interference with the German Empire. Why then did Austria arm herself and plunge Central Europe again into all the horrors of war? Because she thought that Napoleon was so entangled in the mountains of Spain that she could strike him a mortal blow before he could recover himself.

I have never seen, from the most prejudiced writer, any defence of this violation of a sacred treaty on the part of Austria. Napoleon was enraged, and stigmatized it, "A war without an object, and without a pretext." "Thrice, said he, "has Austria perjured itself." Yet how few Americans in reading the description of the battles of Aspern and Wagram fail to utter exclamations of horror against Napoleon, as though on his soul rested the blood of the slain, whereas he was enraged beyond measure at the perfidy of Austria which forced him to recall his troops from Spain.

The treaty of Vienna followed, by which Austria lost extensive possessions. France gained territory—what other indemnification could she receive for such an expensive war, forced on her in the face of a sacred treaty, and what other punishment could Napoleon inflict on a perjured nation, that like an assassin, had endeavored to stab his empire in the dark? Napoleon is not to blame for wresting territory from Austria as a compensation for the losses of war, but for not dismembering her, dividing her three crowns, thus prostrating her independence and power forever.

I have not time to go into the changes produced in Switzerland and Italy, besides I am not defending Napoleon's acts, except when the simple question as to the authors of a war is to be settled.

Thus far it is easy to fix the guilt of nearly every war that desolated Europe for so many years. They were brought about by some or all of the allied powers under the pretence of guarding against danger or to get back territory which had been ceded by treaty.

The next war, the one with Russia, grew out of the irritation of the latter at the great accessions of territory to the French Empire, and from the fear that Napoleon would attempt to reinstate Poland. Leaving aside all other ostensible and real motives, the war would doubtless have been prevented, had Napoleon consented to the demand of Russia, "that the kingdom of Poland should never be established, and that her name should be effaced forever from every public and official act." There were other causes of grievances on both sides, but not enough to have disturbed the peace of Europe, could this have been guaranteed. Napoleon consented to "bind himself to give no encouragement tending to its re-establishment," but he would not go a step farther. The slight to the Emperor Alexander's sister by abruptly breaking off the negotiation of marriage, and the swallowing up of the possessions of the Grand Duke of Oldenburg, his brother-in-law, were among other incitements to hostility; but the fear that this Colossus, who strode with such haughty footsteps over Europe, might yet lay his hand on Poland and wrest from him his ill-gotten possessions, was at the bottom of the warlike attitude which he assumed. This fact which cannot be denied, shows that Napoleon had done nothing that could sanction Russia in breaking that alliance, offensive and defensive, formed at the peace of Tilsit. But France needed but little provocation to justify her in assailing a power that with short intervals had so long waged an unprovoked war against her. Removed so far from the theatre of hostilities, Russia had been able to inflict severe troubles on France while the latter could do nothing in return but crush her armies.

In short, Alexander entered on this war because he anticipated encroachments on his possessions, obtained some fifteen years before by one of the most unholy conquests recorded in the annals of modern civilization. Napoleon was not averse to the war, for he also began to look out for the future, and there could be no better time than now when all Europe marched under his standard, not only to chastise Russia for the injury she had done France, but to prevent her from inflicting it in future. Without doubt there was blame on both sides, but the unprejudiced reader of history will, all things considered, have no hesitation in placing the heaviest proportion on Russia.

But what shall be said of the desolating wars that followed the disasters of the Russian campaign? Austria and Prussia had both entered into a solemn treaty with Napoleon and put their troops under his command in the invasion of Russia, yet no sooner did they behold his army in fragments than with a perfidy and meanness unparalleled in the history of civilized nations, they joined hands with Russia, and rushed forward to strike with deadlier blows an already prostrate ally.

It is generally regarded a point of honor among men never to desert a friend and ally in distress—and to fight by the side of a friend one day against a common enemy, and on the next turn and smite him for no other reason than because bleeding and staggering under the discomfiture he has met with he is no longer able to defend himself, is considered the meanest act of an ignoble soul and the last step to which human baseness can descend. I suppose it will be unnecessary for me to attempt to prove on whom rests the guilt of the battles of Lutzen, Bautzen, Dresden, Culm, Gros Beren, Katzback, Dennewitz, Leipsic, with its awful slaughter, and Hanau—or of those other murderous engagements on the soil of France—of the battles of Brienne, Rothiere, Champaubert, Montmirail, Vauchamps, Monterea, Craon, Laon, and of Paris, unless it is necessary to prove a monarch has a right to defend his crown, and a brave people their own soil. Villainy for once, at least, triumphed, and perfidy and treachery were rewarded with success. Prussia and Austria by falling suddenly on their prostrate ally succeeded in strangling him.

The coalition was successful, and Napoleon robbed of his crown and his empire was sent toElba. It was natural that the monarchs of Austria and Prussia, whose thrones, Napoleon when he held them in his power had respected, should crown their debasement by taking from him his. A few months before they had sworn to defend him against Russia, and now at her request to strip him not merely of his possessions but of his crown, was only doing as violators of their oaths and betrayers of friends have always done.

Like villains of a baser sort, however, they began to quarrel over the spoils they had obtained. There was mustering of armies and all the preparations for a bloody war, but they at length each retired with his portion.

There is but one more war the guilt of which it is necessary to fix before the curtain drops on the public life of Napoleon, and the Holy Alliance has it all its own way on the continent. The manner in which Napoleon mounted his recovered throne was the best title to it he could have had. The heart of the people replaced him there, and as his triumph had been peaceable, so did he wish his reign to be. No one is so insane as to assert that he desired the war that ended in the disasters of Waterloo.

War was declared against him by the infamous coalition which had so often attempted his overthrow. To his offers of peace the allies returned no answer, for they had none to give. His complete destruction would satisfy them, and nothing else. He strove nobly to save himself, but could not. The dead at Quatre Bras, Ligny, and Waterloo are silent but awful witnesses against the tyranny that forced them to struggle for monarchs who were governed solely by ambitious views and unworthy jealousies. The defence set up for the allies that Napoleon would not long be quiet, I have before considered.

To cause sixty thousand men to be slain in order to prevent a nation from declaring war, may do very well at the tribunal of European diplomacy, but before the "court of high heaven," it will meet with a different reception. Besides Napoleon offered to form a treaty of peace, and they could not suppose he could break it with more deliberate faithlessness than England had violated the treaty of Amiens, or Austria that of Presbourg, or both Austria and Prussia their plighted word after the disasters of the Russian campaign. Neither could Russia believe he would grasp any state with more cruel ferocity, and oppress it with heavier burdens than she had seized and loaded Poland. England it is true might be compelled to give up the French possessions in the West Indies which she had seized as a part of her spoil, and the time might arrive when Napoleon would bring to terrible account the faithless allies who had turned on him in his misfortunes, and stripped him of his empire. All this may be very true, and furnish an easy explanation to the war that closed with the night on the field of Waterloo, but in heaven's name charge not the terrible slaughter and suffering that accompanied it to Napoleon. Never in a worse situation to carry on hostilities, he would have signed almost any treaty rather than have risked his throne in a premature struggle. What he might have done in the future, what wars he might have waged, and what guilt he might have incurred, I leave to prophets to determine; but for the war which finished him, and the sufferings attached to it, he is guiltless.

In this review I have touched only on the chief points because I had not space to treat the matter more fully. My motive has been to show that the gallant deeds of the Old Guard, which I have recorded, are not to be classed with those of Caesar's legions. The part Napoleon and his Guard performed is one of the most important in history. The hand of heaven is visible throughout. They were destined to shatter feudalism into a thousand fragments, and no less power than theirs could have done it. Where would have been civil freedom in Europe, without them—where that progress in the knowledge of the people respecting their rights, which has since shorn kings of their pride and taught them civility to their subjects? In struggling for the divine right of kings and the security of monarchies, the haughty and unscrupulous powers of Europe undermined both. Instead of burying republicanism fathoms deep, they sowed dragons' teeth, the fruit of which they are now reaping.

The truth is, our prejudices have all been obtained from English papers and English literature. But if one wishes to know how much these can be relied on, let him turn to the same papers and same authorities, and read the accounts of the war of 1812. If we believe the one history we should the other. It is true, in abiding by this fair rule, we would be compelled to put ourselves in the same category with Napoleon, and look upon our government as alone guilty of that war. By her showing, England never yet was wrong. But alas, history proves that although she declaimed so loudly against Napoleon's grasping spirit, she has since acquired more territory in the Indies than she ever charged him with conquering. Let us beware how we adopt the opinions of the enemies of republicanism as our own, and render all honor to the brave who have borne a part second only to ourselves in the regeneration of all human governments.

In conclusion, I would ask my countrymen to look at the conduct of Russia in the last struggle of Hungary for liberty. What sent the northern hordes against that brave people and laid their liberties and their nationality in the dust? Rest assured the same motive that sent her against the French Republic and afterwards against Napoleon. What now causes Austria to whip and imprison Hungarian ladies and patriots and expel Americans from her borders as if they were degraded criminals?—the same motive that impelled her to break treaties and violate her honor in the effort to overthrow Napoleon, viz., "the security of governments," "to prevent a general earthquake." What induces the king of Naples to fill the prisons of his kingdom with the noblest men in it? The "security of government." What places the continent under a general system of espionage and makes domiciliary visits necessary and suspected persons criminals without testimony?—"securityofgovernment." What causes us to be viewed with a jealous, suspicious eye—our movements watched—our actions misrepresented, and our institutions slandered? "the security of government. What lies at the bottom of the horrible oppressions that are weekly borne to our ears from the despotisms of Europe? The same that lay at the foundation of the perfidy and falsehood, and perjury, and perpetual wars that discrowned Napoleon, and for a while hushed the cry of freedom, that rising from revolutionary France, swept like a whirlwind over Europe. Remember this when you hear of the "balance of power," "security of government," which are terms used simply to cover up the oppressions, and barbarity, and selfishness that have made the thrones of Central Europe for so many ages a curse to mankind. Remember that in siding with feudalism you condemn yourselves.

LEONAUR

ALSO FROM LEONAUR

AVAILABLE IN SOFTCOVER OR HARDCOVER WITH DUST JACKET

THE COMPLEAT RIFLEMAN HARRIS by Benjamin Harris as told to & transcribed by Captain Henry Curling—The adventures of a soldier of the 95th (Rifles) during the Peninsular Campaign of the Napoleonic Wars

WITH WELLINGTON'S LIGHT CAVALRY by William Tomkinson—The Experiences of an officer of the 16th Light Dragoons in the Peninsular and Waterloo campaigns of the Napoleonic Wars.

SERGEANT BOURGOGNE by Adrien Bourgogne—With Napoleon's Imperial Guard in the Russian Campaign and on the Retreat from Moscow 1812 - 13.

SWORDS OF HONOUR by Henry Newbolt & Stanley L. Wood—The Careers of Six Outstanding Officers from the Napoleonic Wars, the Wars for India and the American Civil War, with dozens of illustrations by Stanley L. Wood.

SURTEES OF THE RIFLES by William Surtees—A Soldier of the 95th (Rifles) in the Peninsular campaign of the Napoleonic Wars.

ENSIGN BELL IN THE PENINSULAR WAR by George Bell—The Experiences of a young British Soldier of the 34th Regiment 'The Cumberland Gentlemen' in the Napoleonic wars.

HUSSAR IN WINTER by Alexander Gordon—A British Cavalry Officer during the retreat to Corunna in the Peninsular campaign of the Napoleonic Wars.

NAPOLEONIC WAR STORIES by Sir Arthur Quiller-Couch—Tales of soldiers, spies, battles & sieges from the Peninsular & Waterloo campaingns.

JOURNALS OF ROBERT ROGERS OF THE RANGERS by Robert Rogers—The exploits of Rogers & the Rangers in his own words during 1755-1761 in the French & Indian War.

KERSHAW'S BRIGADE VOLUME 1 by D. Augustus Dickert—Manassas, Seven Pines, Sharpsburg (Antietam), Fredricksburg, Chancellorsville, Gettysburg, Chickamauga, Chattanooga, Fort Sanders & Bean Station..

KERSHAW'S BRIGADE VOLUME 2 by D. Augustus Dickert—At the wilderness, Cold Harbour, Petersburg, The Shenandoah Valley and Cedar Creek.

A TIGER ON HORSEBACK by L. March Phillips—The Experiences of a Trooper & Officer of Rimington's Guides - The Tigers - during the Anglo-Boer war 1899 - 1902.